GRIEF AS I KNOW IT

by

Jandy Chambers

1st Books™
1663 Liberty Drive, Suite 200
Bloomington, IN 47403
www.authorhouse.com
Phone: 1-800-839-8640

1st Books™ UK Ltd.
500 Avebury Boulevard
Central Milton Keynes, MK9 2BE
www.authorhouse.co.uk
Phone: 08001974150

© 2006 Jandy Chambers. All rights reserved.

No part of this book may be reproduced, stored in a retrieval system, or transmitted by any means without the written permission of the author.

First published by 1st Books   12/27/2006

ISBN: 1-5850-0133-3(sc)

Printed in the United States of America
Bloomington, Indiana

This book is printed on acid-free paper.

Having lost five family members to death and having gone through a divorce in a 2 ½ year period beginning at the age of 26, sets the unbelievable journey Jandy Chambers had to embark on. In her book, *Grief As I Know It* takes you through her experiences of her having lost her mother, father, 35 year old sister, brother, grandmother, aunt, a divorce, as well as cancer. Jandy takes you through the events and shares her healing techniques used to not only get through the pain, but turn her experiences into a life changing, positive experience. This book caters to helping others deal with their pain and move forward in life. As the reader turns each page, they will know that Jandy understands and connects with their feelings and knows the trials and tribulations of grief. This combination self-help/autobiography stands out through its honest and vivid accounts of her experiences.

Visit Jandy's Grief Resource Website at www.jandyc.com

I would like to thank Nial Connolly for graciously offering his painting to me as a cover for my book. This piece is entitled, Children Who Die and was painted after he lost his twelve day old nephew. Nial has a wonderful website devoted to his art, music and writing. I invite you to log on and get to know Nial at:

www.yantraimages.com

To God, for without this spirit,
none of this would be possible

IN MEMORY OF:

Jane Anne Barnes Odum
Victoria Elizabeth Odum Reed
John Monroe Andy Odum
Helen Merrill Barnes
Margaret Anne Barnes
John Odum
And part of my right breast

THE END TO THE BEGINNING

An Introduction

There are some mornings when I wake up and it is hard to believe that the people I loved are now gone to a place unknown to me. Within a two and a half year period of time, beginning when I was twenty-six, I lost five family members. Death started to become almost too familiar. Pain came and went in waves and could never be predicted.

I had never experienced loss before and then I received a huge dose within a small fraction of time. Childhood memories popped up in my mind of my mother telling me that she would never die. As childish as it was, even at age twenty-six, there was still an inner belief that my mother was invincible and would never leave me. So when she passed away I had a sense of disbelief, anger, and resentment towards her for having lied to me. "How could she have left me?" I asked myself.

During this two and a half year period I lost both parents, my sister, my aunt, my grandmother and a huge chunk of my heart. At the time I was also going through a divorce. Another death of sorts. I only had one family member left, my older brother John. To my astonishment, my brother too was taken from me by cancer a few years later. It was unbelievable to me in so many aspects that they were gone and I was now left alone without a family to call my own. Yet, I would get one more devastating piece of news. One year after my brother died, I got a phone call that I also had cancer. With each affliction that came I thought that there would be an end to the process, but it seemed to be the beginning of yet another piece of my journey. At the time, I thought it may just be the road to hell. But years later, I realized it was actually the road to a brand new life.

I want to share this journey in hopes that you can find somewhere in your life and in your heart to take your afflictions and turn them into a meaningful journey that will forever change your life and your heart.

THE GOOD OLE' DAYS

My mother and father were entertainers, singing their hearts out all across the United States from town to town, night to night. I have always been proud of the old black and white publicity pictures and newspaper clippings that I have of them. Every chance I got I would show them to my friends, leaving them intrigued and excited about what it must be like coming from a "show business" family. It definitely had its moments, but mostly, the flashy pictures were a front for a very chaotic lifestyle.

My mother was beautiful with her hourglass shape, sexy stage dresses, and a perfectly penciled-in beauty mark that rested on her cheek. My father was handsome and looked like a suave leading man straight out of a 1950's movie. Unfortunately, both were alcoholics.

I loved my family despite a dysfunctional upbringing. The booze, drugs, and of course dad's extra marital affairs were always on my mind growing up. At age seven, I had an ulcer due to the stress of having these people around me and then my parents divorced. My brother, John, was eighteen years older than I was and no longer in the house to protect me. My sister Vicki, who was six years older than me, soon received that task. Unfortunately, she detested it which ensured that she would despise me as well as blame me for having taken her childhood away from her. But these four people were my family, and despite everything, I was not ready for them to die.

My mother grew up on the stage since she was four years old. She was already winning talent shows every week in rural Georgia and actually bringing in more income than her father. He was the town drunk who they would literally have to pull out of the street from time to time. I'm sure a four-year-old bringing in more money than her father during the Great Depression didn't help matters.

I used to love hearing the tales of my mother, who as a young girl lived with reckless abandon. Throughout her youth, she broke both of her legs, one of her arms, her nose twice and also her back. Believe it or not, most of these occurred during separate events. She would tell me stories of playing Batman, and how she would jump off the roof because she thought she could fly. That led to one of the broken legs. There was also the time she was playing cowboys and Indians with a neighborhood boy, but when she was about to jump off a picnic table with her head in a noose, her father caught her in the nick of time before she hung herself.

One of her neighborhood friends (all of her friends were boys) would steal warm biscuits from the window sill when her mother would set them out to cool. My mother got so frustrated that one time she went out into the yard, picked up chicken poop and put it inside the biscuits. I laughed so hard when she told me about the boy biting into the biscuit and running home crying and screaming about what had been done to him. I think that this was the last of the biscuit stealing. This was also the same little boy, (mother told me), who would bury chickens with only their heads exposed, and then run over them with the lawnmower. Mother was never fond of chickens after that experience.

Mother lived a very dysfunctional childhood with her alcoholic father and mentally unstable mother. I believe my mother's attitude of reckless abandon was an escape from this fate she was dealt. My grandmother, who started my mother's show business career, tried to end it early when my mother was six years old. My grandmother decided that what they were doing was evil. She began to mentally snap. She made my mother gather all of her trophies, awards, records and memorabilia and put them in the back yard in a pile. She reluctantly did so as her mother began torching all the beloved mementos. For the next few years, my mother was drug around by her mother to various jails and forced to sing hymnals to the inmates in hopes that they might find reckoning day. My mother was even the one who found my grandmother one time when she had made a suicide attempt unsuccessfully. That followed my mother for a lifetime.

I remember as a child being delighted by the rebellious stories my mother would tell about how her mother would put her in a very frilly dress, and then fix her hair in audacious curls like Shirley Temple for church each Sunday. The tomboy that my mother preferred to be, my grandmother hated. Every Sunday like clock work she would prance her butt outside while her mother was getting ready and she would purposely sit on the lumps of coal and get filthy and then drag her dirty black hands through her curls. I was told she would get the "woopin" of a lifetime....EVERY SUNDAY. You would think that my grandmother would have figured it out, and started to get herself ready first before my mother, but that never happened. Needless to say, mother was a pistol.

But mom had to endure many years in the church unwillingly. I suspect that her unwillingness came because of the forced situation, and the obsessed behavior her mother conducted. To add insult to injury, the pastor tried to make a sexual pass at my mother, harming her emotionally and mentally for the rest of her life. She never forgave him and blamed the church for everything. She could never see further than the pastor's mistakes to forgive God for allowing it to happen. This event would ensure a lack of trust with men as well as trusting others in general for a lifetime, but an even greater need to get the hell out of dodge. And then a few years later, she met my dad.

Dad was also a hand full. He began playing the drums and performing when he was eight years of age. Older friends in bands would sneak him into the back room of nightclubs so that he could play drums for them. As he grew older, he became quite the looker and quite the womanizer. He prided himself in being a "wonderer."

Dad had been abandoned by his father at an early age, and was raised by his hardened mother. I never heard much about his father, and never really knew why he left. His mother had to do whatever it took to make a buck. Desperate for money during the Great Depression, she started making money by reselling cigarettes. She would have just enough money to go buy a box of cigarettes, and then she would turn around and sell them individually at a higher cost. Then she ventured out into buying a few canned goods, and would sell those until she saved enough to rent a small building, where she opened up a grocery store that was eventually fully stocked.

Dad learned from her to be crafty at an early age, although she was not a nice woman. Somehow along the years she received the name "Tommy" and that is always what I knew her as, "Grandma Tommy," who I only got the opportunity to meet once.

Over the years, I would learn that Grandma Tommy was very abusive to my father, often favoring her oldest son over him. Nearing her death, she even told my father that she wished that he had died instead of his brother who had passed away in his forties due to a heart attack. I'm glad I only met her once. But it is amazing how the behaviors and culture would filter down.

My parents met when they were eighteen with both desiring like the wind to get out of town and away from these lifestyles that would ultimately wane on them. They were looking for any excuse. They met of course in a nightclub, and eventually decided to pool their talents (and, well yes, their DNA) to create this family that would become my wind whirl to escape.

From the time they were eighteen to when my mother turned 36, they traveled together doing what they did do best; performing their hearts out for audiences. And they did it well. They were two very talented individuals. My mother even received an offer from Sun Records to record an album, but she turned them down citing that they were a duo, and without pops there was no deal. This was a decision she would later regret. So mom and dad spent many years performing and drinking, an act that would later prove to be destructive to their marriage and to their children.

Mom retired from the road settling in Indiana right before my birth realizing that my sister was ready to enter school and then I would be born and need to be raised. My brother, eighteen years older than me, was on his way to college in Tennessee.

My brother had traveled with my parents on the road all those years being the witness and often the subject of much verbal and physical abuse from my father. Mother mostly looked the other way hoping that this really wasn't the life she was leading. Mom got off the road and dad decided to continue to travel. He continued on well into his fifties making it impossible for us to see him. I was lucky to see him once a year, and there were many collect phone calls. When money was tight and we had no phone, there would be hours at a time standing in the cold and waiting for the pay phone to ring when he had promised he would call at a designated time.

Mother's alcoholism at this point was raging to the point where I remember snowy nights in Indiana waiting on the stoop with my sister outside a local bar while she was inside getting a drink. Better yet, I loved the times when we would go to the old hotel bar in town, and we would sit and talk while she had her cocktail and I would order my "kiddie cocktail." I was all of five or six years old. It's amazing that I never had a drinking problem. However, it would ensure that I would endure a different host of problems as I grew up. Like my mother, I would deal with dysfunctional parents as well as having difficulty with codependence and issues of abandonment. I had a love/hate relationship with my mother. I adored her creative show biz side and I detested the weak and pitiful sides of her. I allowed myself to have both feelings towards her without trying to beat myself up. However, I didn't have that luxury of understanding that as a child.

When I was about seven, my brother recognized the problems my sister and I were enduring and talked my mother into moving to Bowling Green Kentucky where he had settled after college and opened a music store shortly after marrying. My mother had quit drinking right before this time but John knew that we needed more positive direction. This would be the beginning of us trying to make a functional family.

These are the people I knew as my family and without all of the experiences good and bad and maybe even awful, I wouldn't be who I am today. And I really like who I am today. I think the main reason is because I have embraced each event with sheer determination to make something good of it. Or I was going to die trying!

THE UNKNOWN BEGINS

My losses began in late December of 1991 while I was living in Dallas and going through a divorce after five years of marriage. I had moved to Dallas shortly after high school to escape how I knew my life would surely turn out if I stayed. My mother's favorite aunt passed away. I had only met her a couple of times, corresponding with her on and off, but knew her well through my mother. My mother took the news of my great aunt's death extremely hard.

My mother had been ill the last couple of years, and she was in and out of the hospital with emphysema and a tranquilizer addiction. She had given up alcohol years ago, but was still a dry drunk (drunk behavior intact). She had been an alcoholic most of her life, and had experienced difficulty coping as long as I had known her. Mostly, she just feared living. The fear had been cultivated through her childhood living with a drunken father and a manic depressive mother, who had spent time in psychiatric wards.

My mother was named executor of my great aunt's will but due to her own physical and mental condition, she could not carry out the task. I had noticed my mother descending into a downward spiral over those last couple of years, but when my great aunt died, there was a change in her voice and behavior. Shaky and ill at ease, I could sense her fear escalating as she contemplated her own mortality.

My aunt had led a reclusive life. She seldom left home, and so the neighbors would often check on her or bring her groceries. Four days had gone by before she was found. Vicki, my older sister of six years and her husband who now lived in Chicago, took over the duties of cleaning out my aunts' house and executing the proceedings of the will. My brother-in-law had the awful task of cleaning up the fluids and stench left behind. The house was full of antiques and junk to sell or discard, but my sister managed to get through it.

I remember feeling very surprised at my sister volunteering for this dreadful and painful job of taking care of my aunt's estate. My sister had carried around so much resentment all of her life toward everyone in the family. She had always distanced herself from us emotionally and physically, so it seemed strange to me that she so quickly jumped in to help.

My sister had also been witness to much abuse with our alcoholic parents. She was the victim of my father's sexual passes (though never manifested), which surely would destroy any hope of a normal childhood and later would prove to be difficult with establishing trust in relationships. Though she may have seemingly been justified to carry the resentment she held, Vicki knew how to take it to new heights. She had her own way of being sarcastic and standoffish towards those who loved her. She blamed each of us for whatever she had "been through." I remember every time she would come home to visit my shoulders instantly tightened around my ears as if my arms were now earrings. The stress was so thick and uncomfortable being around her. But, all of the sudden, here she was jumping in to help.

I only talked to my mother a couple of times after my great aunt's death. She was not in a cooperative or communicative mood. I had not seen her in a couple of years. The Christmas holiday was approaching and I had to make a decision as to where I would spend it. I wanted to see my mother, but I had not seen my father in twelve years. At the time my mother was still living in Kentucky, my father in Arizona, my sister in Chicago and I was in Dallas. I guess we all wanted to be as far apart as possible.

My father was suffering from autoimmune hemolytic anemia, and was not doing well. I sensed he did not have a lot of time left, so I felt I should visit him. I was afraid I might not get another chance. I flew out on Christmas Eve about a week after my great aunt's death.

My father had re-married soon after he and my mother had divorced. He married the woman he was having an affair with at the time and I had never met her before. She had always been considered the "evil woman." When I was about five years old, my father had used the excuse that he was only able to come into town on Thanksgiving and visit us for a few hours. He claimed to have a gig and needed to get on the road. So, he made his quick get-away after a few hours and a few drinks. That same day, my mother, sister, brother and his wife decided we would go eat Chinese food. I remember sitting at a large round table, and we were all enjoying ourselves until my father suddenly walked in with his arm around "the other woman." It sent my mother into a panic and as for me, I began crying. Mother hustled me into the bathroom as my brother spoke to my father. This would be the end of their relationship. There were many memories like this one that I had to sort through, but I wasn't comfortable not seeing my father ever again, so this forged my decision to go see my him.

When my father and stepmother met me at the airport, he informed me that my mother had called. She wanted to let me know she was back in the hospital for a few days, but not to be concerned. I wasn't. She had been in the hospital so often over the last couple of years that most of the time she was crying wolf and looking for pity.

Mother wallowed in self-pity, not giving herself a chance to be well. Many of her problems were emotionally based. She, like her mother, had spent some time in the psychiatric ward at the hospital. Though it seemed to run in the family, this was one tradition I was determined to stop in its tracks! Everyone had reached out to her many times over the years, but she did not want to help herself. I knew she was experiencing a lot of stress after having lost her aunt the previous week, so I called to check on her after arriving at my father's house.

I could hear the fear and stress in my mother's voice, but I was also very tired of playing the savior. As usual, she played me for the guilt one more time. "Don't worry about me, I'm fine. You have a good time," she stated in her upbeat depressive voice that was clear as a bell. Guilt manipulation. I felt I couldn't do anything right.

When my father initially told me about my mother's call before I had arrived, I remember feeling resentful and angry. I felt this was her way of getting back at me for having gone to visit my father instead of her. So, I blew it off.

I spent a pleasant Christmas day with my father. We got up early and ate a hearty breakfast followed by the opening of presents. We had fun video taping the event and my stepmother stayed in the kitchen all day fixing dish after dish. I just knew I was going to gain ten pounds while I was there. It was good seeing my dad, but it was also strange after twelve years. He looked older and frailer, which disturbed me. I was facing something I had never experienced before but I didn't know the extent of what was to come.

The day after Christmas was spent exploring the Arizona mountains in their truck. The horizons were beautiful and almost unreal. The mountains were enormous and the colors were breathtaking. This amazing landscape was before my eyes, however, I felt detached from its beauty.

An uncomfortable feeling grew within every cell of my body, but I didn't understand why. I knew I was having to adjust to seeing my father after twelve years. I began to feel blasé and started to reflect on my experiences with my parents. My mother was dominating not only my thoughts but also my energy.

My father and stepmother saw my growing discomfort and anxiety. Once questioned, I explained that I had a very bad feeling about my mother, but tried to brush it off. We stopped at a few rest points looking at the beautiful mountains before finding a small diner next to a lake for lunch.

I felt so uncomfortable. I felt restless and my stomach was churning. My uneasy feeling was increasing, and I became even quieter. I knew this made my dad and stepmother worry because I'm sure they were wondering if I was uncomfortable with them. Over time, the uneasy feeling became too much to bare. I requested that we return to my father's home so that I could find some peace in knowing that everything was okay. I just knew I did not feel safe and needed to be somewhere that I could. Traveling back home to Dallas seemed like a really good idea at this point.

Quiet and nervous, I sat on the edge of my seat in the truck as we returned to my father's home. We slowly began winding down the mountains. My body shook slightly, and I felt like a cat wanting to pace back and forth. Every fiber in my body was telling me something was not right and mother was my constant thought.

I had joined Adult Children of Alcoholics about a year before in hopes to begin dismantling some of the dysfunction from my childhood. My sponsor in Adult Children of Alcoholics had taught me that when you cannot handle something to turn it over to your higher power, in my case God. With this in mind, I began a conversation with God.

I told God that I wished he would help my mother find a way to live happily and without regret, to help teach her to learn from her pain instead of suffer. Then I expressed that if she was unable or incapable of finding this, that she be taken from the earth and released from her pain.

After my conversation with God, I felt melodramatic yet glazed over by an uncomfortable haze. I looked at my watch and it was 3:15 in the afternoon. I felt a panic and an instant need to be somewhere safe where I could be in control again. I didn't know at the time why I was having all of these feelings, but all I knew was that I felt very overwhelmed. I tried to attribute it to the fact that I was with my father who I hadn't seen in twelve years and not with my mother.

After what seemed like an eternity, we arrived at my father's trailer. I was trying to be patient allowing them to lock their truck, walk up the stairs, and unlock the door. I didn't want to seem crazy, but I felt as if I was about to explode when I rushed in and saw the message light blinking on my father's answering machine.

I felt dread and yet separated from reality. I had to wait for my father to play the messages. It seemed as if everything was in slow motion as I slowly walked in the front door, laid down the keys, walked to the answering machine, and pressed the play button. Then I heard my sisters' voice on the machine telling me to call her as soon as I got the message. I knew.

I rushed to the phone and quickly dialed her number. When she answered, she told me that she was on the other line and that she would call me right back. I quickly dialed my brothers' phone number and it was busy. I knew.

I sat at the end of the table next to the phone. My stepmother, whom I had just met for the first time that week, was at the opposite end and my father sat next to me holding my hand and looking into my eyes with a reassuring look. I could not look at them. Tears ran down my face as I sat in fear. The pit feeling in my stomach boiled, as I grew increasingly anxious to get confirmation of what my intuition felt I already knew. The phone rang and it was my sister. My mother had died at 3:15 that day as I was sitting out there in God's country. I did know.

All I could do was cry. The anxious feeling in the pit of my stomach was like a bad nightmare coming alive. I was not comfortable anywhere. I tried lying down but could not close my eyes. I tried enjoying seeing my father, but my face was stripped of a smile and I thought in these moments that I would never rest again.

I decided I would return to my mother's home the next day. When I came to visit my father, I had also made plans to see a friend that I had occasionally dated in the past. His parents lived in Phoenix, so he had also come home for the holidays. Before my mother died, we had decided to go out that night. It was painful being with my father and in his home. Around him, I had to face all sorts of realities all at once and right now I could only handle one. Breathing.

I chose to go ahead and go out with my friend. I needed to get away from the reminders, and buy time before I had to leave. When he came and got me, I sat down in his car and told him of my mother's dying that afternoon. He was shocked and speechless. I told him I wanted to go out to celebrate my mother's life, and to step away from the pain for just a few hours before I would have to face it in all its magnitude.

My friend and I went out, and I proceeded to get totally wasted. I don't drink often, so it does not take much. By the end of the evening, I realized my emotions were not going to take the sidelines for any length of time. My friend and I were sitting in the parking lot of a restaurant when all of the sudden I burst into tears and began crying uncontrollably. Then out of nowhere, I began to laugh so hard my sides hurt. Then the tears came again. For what seemed like an hour (but in actuality was only minutes), I cycled between these emotions.

My friend sat there in the car beside me and watched me go through this spiral. He let me do what I needed to in that moment. He did not judge me or tell me not to cry or that I would get over this one day. I felt as if it were a miracle that my friend had been put in the same city at the same time while I had to go through this difficult period. I did not feel it was a "coincidence."

THE LONG ROAD HOME

The next day I proceeded to board the plane for Kentucky for what would be a very difficult and painful experience. I did not even bother putting on my makeup, and I cried the entire trip. I felt sorry for the couple sitting next to me on the plane who questioned me about my distraught state. This was my first experience knowing that it would always be uncomfortable telling others of my loss and that there would be no words to relieve my pain.

I was shocked to get off the plane and find that my brother had come to get me. My brother and I had not gotten along for some time and had not spoken in almost four years. My anxiety was building fast seeing my father for the first time in twelve years which was hard enough, and now I was about to face my brother because of a situation that had just turned my world upside down.

There were many small family squabbles that started our downward spiral, but I topped it off when I wrecked a car that he had co-signed for me. Though I tried to take responsibility for my actions, there was too much anger and too much history in the way for us to work through those issues right then and there. It turned out to be a good excuse to remove ourselves from each other for some time and figure out our roles.

Have you ever looked back and wondered why you were on the outs with someone? This was my situation. I would look back at my relationship with my brother and wonder how we got to this point of not even speaking. It had to do with many years of a dysfunctional family atmosphere and his need to be released from the father-figure role my mother had placed upon him. Also there was my need to grow up and take responsibility for my actions and the beginning of my dysfunctional behavior. He saw my actions taking form, and having been there himself, wanted more for me.

My entire family (including my brother) wanted me to see my father for "who he really was" and give up the relationship because they had abandoned him. In other words, they wanted me to feel about him how they felt about him. I never actually lived with my father however, and never really experienced the outward abuse they did. I needed my father, and they did not understand my position. I had to find out in my own way and in my own time the type of man that he was.

My family would prove to be right in most respects, but there were other situations that were often discounted, such as my mother's role and her responsibility in the years of abuse, neglect and abandonment. Whether physical, emotional or mental, it was always there. I just had to learn it for myself without my mother, sister or brother's experiences influencing me. So, this was a bone of contention for a long time until my mother's death.

At the airport, my brother embraced me, apologizing for the loss I was having to experience. I remember thinking that I must look horrible, and that my face was swollen from the tears over the last twenty-four hours. Even in the face of tragedy, I was still programmed to live up to expectations. That was part of being a "showbiz" family, where every moment is like being on stage. My brother informed me that I was going to stay with him, his wife, my sister and her husband. A sense of panic erupted inside me. These were all individuals that I had not had the best relationship with over the years, and I had little communication with them. Would I ever feel safe again? I wondered. Safety for me was more than 800 miles away in Dallas, where I lived and where I didn't have to deal with any of this or any of them.

Looking back, I can say that it was a gift that my brother picked me up from the airport that day. On the long trip to my mother's house, we each began to express our individual growth over the last few years that we had spent apart. We were discovering that we were now a lot different from the individuals who had not gotten along in the past. An eighteen year age difference between us had brought a lot of distance, but with this simple conversation in the car and a not so simple tragedy, it was the first step in closing that gap. From the experience of my marriage, I was starting to identify negative behaviors in myself that were like my mother that I was beginning change. Things like facing my own fear and dependence on others. My brother seemed more understanding of who I was and more at ease to be around.

Though extremely sad, my mother's death brought my brother and me back together and for that I am grateful. I knew we wouldn't be best friends overnight, but I knew that over time we could develop a relationship that could make us both comfortable. We would eventually build a relationship in which we each had grown individually, and could respect each other for having done so while also celebrating our ability to get away from all the abuse and chaos that had originally torn us apart.

Our first stop was our mother's apartment, where my brother and sister and their spouses had already begun dismantling her life. It was a most grueling and invading task, but after some hugs and tears, I began. I felt as if everyone was watching me. I had to go through and pick out items I wanted to keep for sentimental value or items that simply would be useful to me. There were boxes everywhere with remnants that reflected my mother and who she was.

Within one day, we had my mother's apartment totally empty. In some ways, it almost went too fast, yet it wasn't a situation any of us cared to linger. Getting on with life meant taking care of things as quickly as possible so we could concentrate on remembering our mother and working through our grief.

At one point, we were standing in my mother's bedroom while going through her things when my brother broke down crying. This was something I'd never really seen. I did not know how to comfort him even though we were experiencing the same loss. There was no comfort.

When someone close to you dies, it is almost unbelievable. Literally, there is a feeling of not believing that this person has died. This is one of the reasons why funerals are often crucial to the living who are dealing with the loss. When you see before your eyes that this person you loved has indeed passed away, it often helps with the healing process for some individuals.

The most difficult part of the process was going through her purse. This was saved for last, and had been forgotten about until my brother brought it to our attention. For a woman, it is her most private and personal possession.

We found a gimmicky emergency cigarette in a glass container, and a "No Smoking" sign. She had been trying to quit smoking ever since she had been diagnosed with emphysema. This is what was officially listed as her cause of death. We also found a couple of newspaper clippings and a poem I had written in high school about her singing career, which I had received an "A." I felt especially proud that she carried that poem around with her because it had meant a lot to me when I wrote it.

Mom had struggled during her last few years financially, physically, and emotionally. I didn't understand the depth or the severity of any of them and it was only after her death that her life was opened up and I discovered the secrets that she hid behind.

She was also much sicker than I knew. She hid this fact from me, which incited guilt for not having made the discovery (because of course, I should be all knowing). A high school friend of mine who worked at a grocery store, felt sorry for my mother after seeing her in physical distress when she came into the store. She soon began bringing my mother groceries when she could not manage to leave the apartment. After her death, a neighbor told me stories about my mother being unable to get off of the couch for days, and how she was emotionally hurt by her life. These were all things I wish she had expressed to me instead of hiding them.

I wondered why my mother had not shared all of this with me. It hurt me to know that she had to go through this alone. Yet, I also knew that I had always given her the opportunity to be honest with me, but my mother only knew how to get what she needed through guilt manipulation. For our own collective health, the children had begun to step away from her, and for that, I still have sadness. We could not sacrifice our own survival or behavior for any one any longer.

During the last years prior to my mother's death, we had grown increasingly uncomfortable with each other. She was living in self-pity and blame which took a toll on me. I began to take more responsibility for myself and less for my mother. She had told me she understood my need to see my father instead of spending Christmas with her, however, I still felt tension and disloyalty about my decision. The week before her death, our conversations seemed very stressed.

I talked to her on Christmas day when I was in Arizona visiting my father, which was the day before she died. She was in the hospital, and I rang her room and told her that it was me. She breathlessly yelped, "I can't breathe, I can't breathe," and hung up on me. That was my last conversation with her. Needless to say, I felt devastated by it and I could have easily put myself through a lot of guilt for having taken care of my needs over hers the last few years. I had to quickly realize that it was not my fault or responsibility that she was emotionally and physically ill. Even though I had to release myself from any guilt and remember that she loved me, it still hurt tremendously that it had ended this way.

Individuals who experience conflict with a loved one before their death or who were abused by a loved one will experience similar feelings. These unresolved feelings could hinder their abilities to cope with the death and go on with their life. I found that it was more about forgiving myself for not being perfect than it was about forgiving her actions. I had to remember who she was and the family system she came from that had developed the actions that she had displayed. It didn't always make it easy, but if I could try to remember this principle it would help comfort me that her actions were never intentional.

Even though my mother's official death was listed as emphysema, the doctors could find little wrong with her except her mental condition even after running many tests. The day my mother died my brother had gone to visit her, and had even helped her with some breathing exercises. The nurses and doctors had said that she was breathing fine that day, and that she was being upgraded to a step-down unit for patients who were getting ready to go home. Yet my brother had seen a different look in her eyes that day. A look of a child. A look of despondence.

Her eyes were glazed over, and she said little. My brother sensed her neediness, and he left the hospital wondering what he could do for her and feeling helpless.

We were later told that right before she died the nurse came in and checked her vitals, which were fine. By the time my brother got home, (over an hour away), a nurse had left a message on his answering machine that my mother had passed away. It was so insensitive of the nurse to have left such a painful message on an answering machine!

My brother told me that when he went back to her apartment after learning of her death, he found on the kitchen table a list of preparations and requests in the event of her death. It was as if she already knew and had chosen to die. I do believe she chose her death. Mentally and emotionally, it was too difficult for her to live, and there was too much from her past to overcome, but she no longer had the energy to try.

After closing out my mother's apartment and loading up my brother's van, we had dinner at a local restaurant before driving back to his house. It was getting late and we were all exhausted. At dinner, I felt the need to let everyone know about my divorce which was another loss I was also grieving. I felt somewhat uncomfortable about telling them because I was afraid they would view me as a failure. Being in a family of "entertainers" it was very competitive between us all. Yet, I still wanted to be honest and was hoping for some emotional support. They said their regrets to me, and then it was back to the business of my mother. I couldn't expect much in emotional support after having been apart from them for so long. I was just looking for understanding from my sister and brother and received little. I think they both felt like I had made a mistake by marrying in the first place. I brushed it off pretty quickly as if I hadn't brought it up and went about dealing with the grief.

After dinner, my brother-in-law and sister decided they would drive my mother's car back to my brother's house. This was another painful trip. Every few miles, the car would break down. The floorboard of the car had huge rusted holes, and my mother had been unable financially to maintain her car. I felt so much sadness that my mother had had to live this way and could not even afford a reliable source of transportation. We eventually had to leave the car on the side of the road and have it towed the next day. I think that was the longest day of my life.

The hospital sent my mother's body to the town where my brother lived an hour away. She was to be cremated, but I couldn't believe this was all taking place. I was still going through the motions wondering when I would wake up. That night, I was about to spend my first evening in my brother's house with a family I had not gotten along with in years. I brought my suitcase into the house, setting it off to the side of the living room. I plopped down and opened it and begun making myself busy rummaging through my belongings for no apparent reason except to avoid my discomfort with everything that had taken place in the last twenty-four hours.

I didn't really feel welcome or that I belonged in my brother's house even though they had informed me I would be staying with them and told me which bedroom to take. I felt like an outsider scrambling for safety, yet there was none to be found. I knew I was just going to have to wing it moment by moment and remember that it was okay to just be me. Sometimes I had to reassure myself even though I felt like I was lying to myself. There were times when I wanted to feel like everything was going to be alright but I wasn't totally sure.

It was an interesting relationship with my mom. She was a very strong woman in a lot of ways. At least that is the image she portrayed to others but behind closed doors she was very weak. She often relied on my brother, sister and me as if she were the child and she would go through terrible bouts of "poor pitiful me" moments. My sister always felt like she raised my mother instead of the reverse. I remember one day my sister was so fed up with my mother constantly talking about how if it weren't for her children, she would commit suicide. My sister walked over to the bed stand where my mother kept her 38 pistol and picked it up and handed it my mother. My sister told her, "go ahead, get it over with. I'm tired of listening to your threats." It's unimaginable today to think about. My mother could be a fun person at times. There were two definite personalities she could display. We loved going to yard sales together and of course listening to all her great stories and she was considered the "cool" mom by my friends. Beknownst to them what it was like in the dark. So it was devastating to think about burying her and not being able to fix all of these things for her.

The next day we arrived at the funeral home, and began signing papers and getting copies of the death certificate. My sister was then handed the cardboard box that housed a black plastic box that contained a bag of my mothers' ashes. Sixty-four years of my mother's life could now fit into my cupped hands and I could see and feel the pieces of bone. It was too bizarre for words.

I have come to learn that when experiencing such an upheaval, people tend to have very diverse feelings arise. We cried, we fumed, we felt resentful, angry, and we also laughed. Standing outside the funeral home with the ashes sitting in my sister's hand, my brother walked up to her, leaned over placing his ear close to the box, tapped on the box and said, "Mother, Mother, are you in there?" We all began laughing. We had to find some humor in this somehow. We remembered the good times as well as the bad, all the time laughing, crying and knowing that we all truly loved our mother in our own way.

The decision had to be made about how we would disperse the ashes. One of her requests on the paper found on her kitchen table was that she did not want a funeral or formal arrangements. Together, we decided to disperse them on my sister-in-law's property in a creek in the woods.

My mother adored the 1962 Cadillac she had driven for years. She always said that if she died we should just put her in the Cadillac and push it over a mountain. A true die-hard Cadillac lover! Well, what I had in mind was a little less dramatic. My brother had a Cadillac just like hers sitting in his garage, and I made the suggestion that we drive it to take her ashes to the creek. Everyone instantly agreed that this would make her happy, and so we were off for yet another painful trip.

It was just the five of us at the creek. Me, my brother, his wife, my sister and her husband. Dad had not been involved with the rest of the family for some time, and so therefore he stayed informed only through our conversations. We each held the ashes and said something about my mother and her contributions and the sacrifices she had made such as caring for us being a single mother and working two jobs at times. My mother loved cats and her house was full of cat knickknacks. She admired cats for their strong independent attitudes and wanted to be like them. So, the last thing I said to her before I released her was to "keep on prowling." My sister then walked over to the creek and began pouring the ashes into the water.

Everyone except my brother embraced each other as we walked away from the creek. A few minutes later my brother called us back over to the flowing water where he had kept to himself for a few minutes. He said he wanted to make sure he was not seeing things before he showed us something.

We walked back over to the creek, and all looked down to where my sister had just poured the ashes. I said, "Oh my God, they are cats." We were all in disbelief, but before our eyes the ashes had taken shape on the rocks and in the water. It was three cats. You could clearly see the three images. I knew from this experience that my mother was telling me that she was fine and everything was going to be okay. This seemed like her signal to us.

I don't normally live my life looking for strange things to occur. But, after knowing that my mother had died before I was told, and upon seeing these cats in her ashes, it reinforced my beliefs in God and my intuition. I did not grow up religious and my mother kept us away from church. But as I divorced and started to recognize my dysfunctional behaviors I started experiencing a natural progression in my belief for God and it strangely grew stronger as I went through these tragic events.

Over the next few days, my brother and I made amends for our past conflicts. On some days I feel my mother died for this purpose. My relationship with my brother had caused my mother a lot of pain and grief, but now all of her pains were gone including this one. I have learned that life is too short to hold onto anger and resentment. I would be able to return to Dallas with a new hope of a new relationship with my brother. We didn't exactly discuss the infractions we had in our relationship but it was as if we were being able to let go and move on.

It was a time of emotional upheaval as I mourned for my mother, thought about my aunt who also just passed away and my divorce was also being finalized. I already had enough to worry about, but during the trip home back to Dallas I had discovered that my brother had not been doing well physically.

One of the things I can say is that the gene pool is definitely tainted in my family. My brother had been ill on and off for many years. He was born a sick child as my mother was in labor with him for two days before he came out as what they call a blue baby with a lack of oxygen. He had severe asthma his entire life, and began taking daily steroids to breath and function, although this lead to another host of medical problems for him. It didn't help that he was obese most of his life. After my mother passed, he had to undergo major surgery in which we almost lost him several times. He had been told twenty years earlier that he had between six months to one year to live. I had always feared my brother's death, but he was always a fighter and once again he evaded death.

A few months went by and I felt as if I was working through my grief. My divorce was proceeding, yet I was overcome by a lot of pain for all of my losses. One fortunate thing I can say is that even though my husband and I were divorcing, we have always remained friends. There were no hard feelings, just lessons. We learned many things from one another to assist ourselves individually in overcoming each of our family dysfunctions. At the time of our marriage, he needed a mother figure and guide, and I was good at playing the role which also would ensure a new form of dysfunction. Overall, it gave each of us a foundation for growth, but we definitely had a different relationship than most people. We remained such good friends that after our divorce, we moved out of our one bedroom apartment and into a two bedroom and became roommates. Okay, I know it was strange, but it worked for a short time until we each were able to go our separate ways with different partners. But he was there for me a lot during the deaths.

I learned in that marriage that I had adopted many of the dysfunctional patterns from my family and it gave me the opportunity to examine them at their worst and make a conscious decision whether I would want to work those issues out or stay in denial. I chose to grow and overcome them. I also learned that family or not, or married or not, you can still get along and be respectful of one another's differences and still be there for each other.

One day in my ex-husband's presence, I was having an extremely difficult time grieving for the loss of my mother. I was lying on the couch sobbing so hard that I began gasping for air. He literally had to come over and shake me to my senses to get me to start breathing again. My world and my foundation had been shaken to the core.

So much was happening in my life as I was grieving for so much loss. On top of that, I had just started a new job two weeks after my mother died. I must have been insane to accept a new job at this time, but I was so numb that I figured what the hell. I was now working as an Executive Assistant to four cardiovascular surgeons where I ended up staying with for six years. I tried transitioning into a "normal life."

A few months later, I received a phone call from my stepmother. My father was in the hospital, and was not expected to survive. I flew out to Arizona to be with him. Unlike my mother, my father was a real fighter, and no one, including the doctors, could believe that he lived another year after the visit I made to see him. But, a year and a half after my mothers' death, my father passed away.

Again, there was no funeral or formal service and he was also cremated. I felt as if I had tied up all the loose ends with my father during my last trip, so I decided there was no need to go back to Arizona. His wife and her kids had planned a ceremony much like the one we had for my mother. I had only met these people a couple of times, and felt my place was to stay at home since I had no real need to be there. However, my grief process once again went back to square one.

Like my mother, I also had many issues that seemed left undone with my father. He had spent most of my life lying to me about why he constantly cheated on my mother or why the child support checks he would write to me were bouncing or why he was too busy to come visit me. He could never follow through for his family and there was always an excuse. He never admitted that he was an alcoholic, and claimed that he could stop at any time. But of course he never did stop drinking.

As I got older, more stories came to light about my father. They ranged from him being connected to the mafia to him being a hit man to his indulging in drugs and threesomes with women as well as men. Who knows how much of it is true? He had a fascination with lying and he created a life that was more glamorous than the one he was leading. At age eight, I got into a fight with him on the phone and he told me he was going to put a "hit" out on my mother. Wow, those were quality days! I look back and see the magnitude of the dysfunction. What is scary was that for me growing up like this was normal for me. Normal is what you know at the time. Whether healthy or not, it is what it is and a child does not know any better. So, you can imagine after his death my feeling a sorrow that I would never know many truths about his life.

By this time, sorrow and grief had consumed me. I began to feel like things would never return to normal. I couldn't even remember how "normal" felt, (if I ever knew considering my childhood). Even though I felt an over-abundance of grief, there was also a part of me that felt relief that my mother and father had passed. I know this may seem awful to most people, but I had so many problems growing up because of their dysfunctional behaviors. They were unhappy being here on earth and the family suffered much heartache through their actions. Coming from two alcoholic parents who were nightclub entertainers had always been challenging, but now that they were gone, there would be less conflict in my life. I looked forward to the "peace," but it didn't take away my pain and sadness.

Over the years, I had often experienced strained relations with each of my family members. Alcohol, drugs, and dysfunctional behavior that ranged from verbal to emotional abuse made for a crazy upbringing and a strange existence for many years. With the help of Adult Children of Alcoholics and a sponsor, I was able to reassemble my life and become an individual who could have healthy relationships with other people. My sponsor taught me how to break the dysfunctional pattern I had been taught as a child. I thank God for my beginning this work before the death of my parents occurred because it kept me sane during these tragedies.

During all of this grief, I received massage work from a woman who does emotional integration body work. She taught me how to release my sadness, loneliness, anger, and the hundreds of feelings I experienced surrounding my childhood and the deaths. I hate to think where I would be without this woman's help, and she was definitely put in my path to see me through my grief. She wouldn't let me get away with hiding my feelings, and made a comfortable place for me to do whatever it took to get through these emotions (whether it was to yell, scream, kick, hit a pillow or simply cry). The only way to work through the pain is to work through the emotions and to express each one of them in their entirety.

After a few months, I really felt as if the cloud of death was passing. But then there was a knock on the door and I opened it to find that it was storming.

RUN FOR COVER,
HERE COMES THE STORM

My brother, sister, and I were all experiencing fatigue, depression, sadness and other emotions while absorbing my mother's death. My sister, however, seemed to be having a lot of difficulty handling it all. More and more, she seemed profoundly depressed and detached, but I really didn't think much about it because we were all experiencing difficult emotions.

My sister had always been moody, and I had seen her in and out of modes similar to her current behavior. My sister lived in Chicago, so I also had a hard time assessing her situation. Due to a multitude of problems we had over the years, we didn't visit each other often. We had periods in our relationship where we didn't communicate at all. But, there were also periods where we bonded because of our dysfunctional childhood and talked frequently. It all depended on where Vicki was at with her anger, and how much she was willing to let me and others into her world, (but rarely into her heart).

My sister called me at home approximately eight months after my father died, and told me she needed to talk to me about something very important. I remember I was sitting on the couch with my new boyfriend mindlessly watching a program on the television.

I didn't have a clue about what she was going to unload on me. She told me she had been HIV positive for five years. I couldn't believe what I was hearing, yet somehow it felt familiar. Too familiar. I kept my composure, letting tears stream down my cheeks, while I listened to her rationalize why she had waited five years to tell me. She told me that she had felt in the past that I had been too immature to handle such news. I met this statement with a lot of rage that I held back from her.

I felt so betrayed, and once again, so much like I wasn't really a part of this family. My brother had known the entire time, but my sister had sworn him to secrecy. I was very angry with him for not having told me. I respected his ability to live up to his word but was very saddened by the fact that our family could not come together during such crisis. I still think about the time I could have spent with her while she was feeling healthy, if she had only told me of the diagnosis.

She denied being sick, yet weeks later I learned she was already in the AIDS stages and losing her bladder control along with her muscle movement. The condition grew worse quickly, yet the time seemed to pass slowly. Sometimes, I felt like I was watching my life go by as if I was looking out of a window. It felt so unreal. My friends and co-workers were shocked about what was happening in my life, and it grew difficult for me to meet new people because of my circumstances. People always ask questions about your life when they are trying to get to know you, but mine seemed to be going to hell in a hand basket and I could overwhelm someone quickly with the details.

My sister had lived a very turbulent life. She had taken all of her childhood pain, and rolled it into a lifestyle that she hoped would take her out of the reality that she detested. Vicki left home at the ripe age of sixteen to dance in New York City. She had hopes of being a great dancer, but the reality was that she became a great waitress and an even greater drug addict. Her drugs of choice were cocaine and men and her reality was even more skewed because she became involved in a relationship with a man that she would not admit was gay. He was also a ballet dancer, whom she was involved with on and off for years.

She eventually managed to get herself off drugs once she left New York for Chicago, but she would never get this man out of her blood. Literally. He died from AIDS, and left her blood tainted. Unfortunately, Vicki had always been in a great deal of denial throughout her entire life and could not bring herself to tell or admit to anyone how she had gotten AIDS. But, we all knew because it was obvious. I felt sad for her that even as she was facing death, she still could not be honest with herself.

I flew to Chicago to see my sister as I was once again experiencing a dreaded mission. I have experienced a lot of flying in my life under most unpleasant circumstances. My sister could barely speak or walk at this point, and she relied on her husband for everyday care.

Vicki had lost the capacity to walk unassisted at this point. This meant she had to rely on someone else to bring her food, to drink, bathe her, and even take her to the bathroom. She lay all day on the couch that was also her bed, and she wore diapers due to the lack of bladder control.

I saw the desire in my sister's face to get out of the house so the next day, after her husband left for work, I went down to the basement to get her wheelchair, and took it around to the front of the house. There were about ten stairs leading up to their porch.

I pulled my sister up, and set her back against the couch so that she was propped up. Then, after many tries I got a coat on her. It was as if I was dressing a lifeless child because she couldn't help me. I struggled and struggled, trying to move her arms about in a way that would enable me to slip the coat on. At one point, we both began laughing hysterically at my sorry attempts.

Once I got the jacket on her, it was time for the hard part. I lifted my sister up, propping her weight on me and slowly walked her to the porch. (Take into consideration that we are the same height and weight and all she was capable of was a very slight shuffle.) I eventually managed to help her to the top step. I needed to rest a minute, and I wasn't quite sure how I was going to get her down the stairs. I was just so damned determined that she was going to spend some time outdoors being able to see and hear the birds she had always loved.

After resting for a moment, I got up behind her and slipped my arms underneath hers. I pulled her up and then set her down on the next step. Then, I would move each leg down a step farther. One by one, we forged down the stairs, her on her butt and me pulling her with all my energy, not thinking about my own body. Once again, I performed the task of pulling her up and placing her into the wheelchair. Mission accomplished, so I thought.

I wheeled her around the neighborhood and there was a nice chill in the air. It was a very pleasant day, and thankfully, the birds were singing everywhere. My sister looked around and took in everything. I looked at her childlike face, and was struck with so much pain that it felt like a knife in my heart.

When it became time to take her back inside, I almost felt like panicking when I realized that I had to get her back up the stairs. So, once again, I started the task. I placed her on the bottom step, got behind her and pulled her up each step, (placing each foot up one step each time that I moved her). After that long haul, we were finally in the house, with our coats off and I was sitting down amazed at how insane I could be at times. But my insanity came out of love and hope.

I don't know if this was her last visit outside, but I wouldn't be surprised. So, I am still grateful for the strength and tenacity that allowed me to do what I did. Later that night, I woke up in the middle of the night with my back and shoulders in excruciating pain. Every muscle was sore and heated and I could barely move.

I got up at six the next morning, got dressed and walked into a Chicago suburb, which was across some railroad tracks, under a bridge, and not exactly in the safest neighborhood. I was desperately searching out a bottle of pain relievers. Not only had I risked my body by moving her, but I was now risking my own life for relief from the pain. The grief and exhaustion I was feeling because of the deaths that had occurred (and the fate of my sister) had left me feeling careless.

Many emotions such as fatigue, sadness and disbelief were running through me and I wanted to do more, yet I could not. I felt helpless. Nothing I could say or do would help her, but I had to contemplate making amends with her for past childhood wounds. I was frustrated that I couldn't give up my job or take enough time off to stay with her until she passed. Unfortunately, I still had to run my life and pay my bills, which really pissed me off.

Vicki was also mentally deteriorating, and I could see in her eyes that she did not want to be a burden. I felt somewhat satisfied with what I was able to accomplish while I was there, even though it was a heart wrenching experience.

Vicki and I had an interesting relationship. She never liked me, but she never gave me a chance either. From the day I was born, she had resented me. She admitted that fact to me when she was in her twenties, and she had finally come to the realization that she resented my birth for disrupting the attention she was receiving. She was the queen of the house until I arrived, and then she felt I was the competition. It got even more difficult once my mother's drinking got worse, leaving Vicki with the task of taking care of me, (I was a toddler).

Vicki did save my life one time when I became very ill with a high fever, and my mother was too drunk and passed out to take care of me. Vicki bathed me and fed me popsicles, doing whatever she could to get the fever down. So, from the age of six and for many years to come, Vicki got the task of taking care of a child she resented. This must have been hard for her.

I remember one day when we were all at home, and mother fell down in the tub. I screamed out, "Mom's drunk again." Now, take into consideration that I was about five years old and that day, I got the "woopin" of a lifetime. She felt like I had been disrespectful. As these individuals were dying one by one, all of these memories began to flood my brain.

I really thought nothing else could possibly happen at this point. Then, I got word from my brother that my grandmother had died, (my mothers' mother). Like my aunt, I had only met her a few times, but I had corresponded with her on and off during my entire life. After her death, I really mourned my loss of never having had a complete family, and the opportunities that were now gone forever. I started to understand that I was losing them all, except for my brother, and of course I constantly worried about his health. He was the one that doctors had told years ago that wouldn't make it past thirty.

A few weeks later, I took a second trip to see my sister. This time she was totally paralyzed and basically comatose. She lay in her hospital bed in the middle of the living room staring at the wall but unable to move or speak. There was not even a glance from her eyes, and there was no way of communicating with her. I had no idea if she understood that I was there or not. I have to believe that she did.

My sister lay lifeless, eyes open, and her hair matted. Her nails were tinged with a yellow discoloration that looked like iodine. Her mouth and teeth were coated with a white and yellow film that was lightly brushed each day with a device that looked like a sucker. Cards from friends were tacked to the wall next to her hospital bed, and we put together hanging mobiles to hang over her bed for her to gaze upon. I was at a loss for something respectable I could do for her besides just simply being there.

My brother-in-law gave me the terrible task of going through her things, and discarding what I did not want to take. Once again, I had to encounter a task that seemed very imposing. Somehow, I found the energy and courage to take care of her things.

I sat beside her bed reading from books and simply holding her hand. I didn't know what to say as encouraging words seemed ridiculous and good-byes seemed too hurtful. It was so painful leaving her behind. I will never forget walking out of that house realizing that this would be the last time I would see her and there wasn't a damn thing I could do about it. Approximately two weeks later, on August 14, 1994, she died.

It is very painful watching someone you love slowly die as if the lights in the room are dimming. With both my father and sister, I had to go through this painful process. Strangely, they both experienced very similar deaths, losing brain capacity, and ultimately falling into a comatose state before death.

My father started losing his ability to speak, remember, and comprehend things. He then slowly lapsed into a coma and died. I will never forget the last conversation I had with him. He was in the hospital and his wife had to hold the phone for him to speak. I had to tell him who I was and I felt so incredibly uncomfortable. What do you say to someone who is obviously about to die and knows it? I told him that it was time for him to get better and that I had things I wanted us to do. We told each other we loved one another and that was our last conversation.

The shutting down of my sister's body and mind seemed to be as agonizingly slow as it was with my father. For several months, she could not walk and she talked less and less. I would look at her as she would look at me, and in our eyes we both knew her fate. It felt painful, confusing, and I had to fake being "cheery" with her. Like my father, her brain malfunctioned before her body quit.

It is hard to understand why death can come to nice individuals in such a cruel manner. Even though my father had not been the best person while he was living, I still felt the way he died was unjust. My sister was only thirty-five, and had contributed so much to others, which brings up the question everyone wants to know, "Why did this person have to die?" Then there is also the question that lies deep within us coated in fear: "When am I going to die?"

This was a fear of mine in the beginning stages of my grief. It was a knee-jerk reaction. I had to try to remind myself just because my family members were dying that did not mean that I would immediately follow. I could either spend my life contemplating my own death or I could actually try to live it and experience happiness. I knew that the grieving and sadness was not fun, so I decided that I did not want to live my life that way. I definitely did not want to keep re-experiencing pain and fear. Through my faith, I have also come to understand that death should not be seen as a bad thing. It is a privilege to be with God and to be brought home to a secure haven without the worldly concerns I was experiencing in these moments. Not that I wished for my death, I just came to accept its inevitable nature, and this isn't easy to come by. It didn't happen right away for me. There were times I was scared that I would be next and I had to give myself a reality check or call someone who would.

During the last year of these events, my relationship with my first post-divorce boyfriend was already deteriorating. I found it difficult to find happiness in our relationship when I was going through so much pain. He worked and also went to school day and night, so he provided me with little support. This left me even more empty and in need of comfort and love. My heart ached with loneliness, feeling left alone in the world after our breakup on top of the deaths. At this point the only family I had left was my brother and his wife who lived in Kentucky.

During this time when I lost my family, I was still working as a medical secretary for the cardiovascular and thoracic surgeons. Their office was attached to the hospital where they worked. Often, I would have to run errands at the hospital for one of the doctors, and there were days when I found this to be a very difficult task.

Walking through the corridors of the hospital and passing the faces of the sick and seeing the rooms filled with medical testing equipment often pushed my memories back to my losses. I would grit my teeth as I walked to my destination, fighting the tears and the memories until I could get back to the office. So many things in my life were reminders of my loss. Holidays were brutal. Nothing was safe.

I remember times walking down the street, shopping in the mall, or inside the grocery store when I would look into the faces of passersby and wondered what was going on in their world. I wondered if they could even imagine the pain I was going through and I wanted to tell everyone about my pain. I needed to share it, but the few I told didn't understand the depth of my pain and the despair that I felt. I wanted to yell from the rooftops what had happened to me and I needed the world to embrace me.

FACES OF LIFE AND DEATH

During this time, I learned that death doesn't know mercy or kindness. Death doesn't care about how you're going to feel about it. At least that is what I felt. I couldn't stop death from happening and so I felt it unkind. I knew this feeling because death had taken my entire family. That was not only unkind to me but ruthless! Death is a process that starts as soon as we're born, and it is something we have to live with. If you don't face death you don't face life and with each adversity, more questions appeared and were eventually answered though not quickly. How can something so basic be so complex?

I understood that the only way to understand the death process was to experience it, but, I wasn't quite willing to die yet. The closest I could come was through my personal losses. So, needless to say, I was becoming quite a pro. Through my experiences and my spirituality, I began to gain knowledge and insight into loss and the feelings of grief. However, I will not exactly understand death until I die.

Unless one has a fascination or special interest in death, I do not believe that death is something individuals think about until we are faced with it. Death is a taboo subject to many. I assert that most people are fearful of death, and therefore don't want to face it (and honestly, until we have to, do we really need to?). I certainly learned this sentiment going through all of these deaths. People were often very uncomfortable talking to me about it because they wanted to fix it for me, but they didn't know how. There was nothing they could do, and it left them feeling helpless. People often will say stupid things because they don't know what to say. I had to learn great patience with people.

I remember during the deaths that I had a roommate who had never experienced any major event in her life. She even teased me that she came from a "Beaver Cleaver" family. So, from her vantage point, I just looked like a highly emotional person who was blowing everything out of proportion. What she didn't understand was that the depths of my world were being ripped out from under me, and because I didn't have a "normal Beaver Cleaver" family, I also mourned not having a family that was there for me.

I know that before I had experienced loss, I really hadn't faced my fears of dying. I had no reason to, but my life was profoundly changed one day while going about my day- to-day normal business. I had imagined my parents dying, but nothing prepared me until it actually happened. I saw my sister and me growing old together in our rocking chairs on a porch somewhere. Not that this was a realistic thought with our background but I could have never imagined her death. I had plans with all of them before they died, and I wasn't finished with any of them.

When it came to losing my family, I would sometimes find myself wishing for just five minutes of completion time with each of them or even just one individual. It is too bad that we can't choose one thing in life that we can completely control. Some people might choose to be able to control their weight but I would want to control the time with my loved ones right before or after their death so I could be complete with them.

It was still hard to believe that these individuals were gone and that there would not be one last visit or conversation. In an instant, I couldn't call them and I wouldn't be called. There were times when that thought ticked me off, and I would become angry for having it all happen to me. But I knew in order to function, I had to get out of that mindset quickly each time I felt it. I allowed myself those moments to be angry, but then I got over it.

One has to choose for themselves how they will grieve. The actual grieving process seems to be different for everyone, and although it is hard to believe, we will have to integrate it into our lives.

We logically know we are going to die someday, but because we are alive now, it is hard to believe that one day we will face our fears and die. We will be taken from our loved ones, and they will grieve for us and not understand why we have died. Most of my life I have heard that death is natural, however, it doesn't feel natural when one day someone you love is within reach and then they are not. We may consciously know it will happen, but nothing can prepare us for it. Even after all I had experienced, I wasn't ready for my next adversity, whatever that may have been. We also know and understand that we don't go through life unscathed.

I found that there was no schedule for my grieving. Grief just popped up at the most unlikely times, and in the most inconvenient places such as at the grocery store or when I'm having lunch with someone. While shopping I would see some trinket that would remind me of my mother such as something with a cat on it because she loved cats. This would bring up the grief again.

I don't believe there is a required way a person must grieve because every individual's grief process is different. There are definitely feelings we all experience, and also things we can do to help ourselves process our emotions. But, no person or book or self-help tape can tell you how it will exactly play out. That pissed me off too because I wanted answers, but it did help to know that I was not alone. For me, I had not experienced a death until age twenty-six. At age twenty-nine, and five deaths later, I unfortunately felt somewhat like a pro.

Grieving is not just a process of death, but also can include a major change or loss that can occur in our lives (such as my divorce and the loss of my boyfriend). The feelings I experienced during the ending of those relationships felt similar to the feelings I went through with the physical deaths of my family members.

When you lose someone, you not only lose the person, but also the dreams and hopes you had created with that person which can no longer be fulfilled. I found that at this point if I wasn't conscious about my feelings that depression and hopelessness would occur. Needless to say, no one wants to be stuck in grief for an extended length of time. It can begin to effect your daily life and overall well being. Personally, I didn't want to get stuck in this for anymore time than what I needed to get over it.

Because I went through so many deaths in such a short period of time, I experienced overwhelming sadness and wouldn't know whom to grieve first, so I would cycle through feelings toward several individuals at one time.

It was very powerful and very frightening, and at times I felt I couldn't possibly cry anymore and then all of the sudden I'd be bawling. There were times I would feel complete in my grieving process only to find that it would start all over again. I've always heard on TV and read in books that all of those emotions and feelings are normal, yet still painful. I had also learned through my years of dealing with a dysfunctional family that I had a choice in how I could handle the situation. I could take it negatively and let it hold me back, or I could take all of this and make something useful out of it.

With each death I experienced, I had several major lessons to learn that were a positive influence in my life. I wish we could choose how our lessons come to us, (thus there would be no tragedy in the world), but we must find our strength through these situations. I learned that I was stronger than I thought. I learned that I can grow from tragedy and become a better person because of it. I learned how to be independent and still allow myself to rely on others. I learned that I can cry and laugh at the same time and that is alright. Some of the lessons I can't explain to you. Some of them are such deep changes in myself and who I am that there aren't words to express it. I have to say that I've learned to be proud of myself for being able to handle such tragedies. It's kind of funny that that is what I get to be proud of myself for but I guess sometimes we don't get a choice.

I began to ask myself, "How can I turn this from a negative to a positive?" "What lessons did this person leave on the earth for me and others to be able to lead a happier, more fulfilled life?" "How can I use these lessons to enrich my life and the lives of others around me?" Not everybody has to write a book, but there are many ways to create a positive from a negative situation.

Unfortunately, the deaths of my mother and father were one more nail in my sister's coffin. She would never have the opportunity to fix things with either of them, and her relationships with my parents were very poor at the time of their deaths. I think this ate at her mind and her body, which increased the onset of the illness in her system. But Vicki was always too resentful and full of anger to let go long enough to accept any of us for who we were. I understand it was hard for her to forgive, and I also don't believe in forgiving and forgetting, per se. Let me explain.

First of all, you can never forget if a person has hurt you. As much as we would like to forget, the subconscious remembers and forgiving is tricky. It is often relevant to the situation at hand. If someone takes some item from your home and they come to you seeking forgiveness, it may be easier to forgive them for their indiscretion. But when someone you trust such as a parent makes a sexual pass at you or has physically hit you, it is much harder to forgive.

I know God wants us to forgive people for their actions. I also know God wants us to forgive people for their thoughts. I wish it were as simple as saying, "Okay, I will do that," but human emotions are a like a big hundred-year-old oak tree with deep roots embedded in the soil. When someone comes along to remove that tree, it becomes very difficult to uproot because of all of those long veins that have intricately wound themselves around the earth. That is anger and sadness for us and also the forgiving process. It is hard to uproot all of those feelings rooted in us and freely let go.

So, if we have searched our hearts and tried as hard as we can with God's help to forgive these individuals and yet cannot do so, I think there is only one thing we can do. Ask God to forgive us for not being able to forgive. He has actually already done that, and he has forgiven us for our indiscretions.

Though we may not be able to forgive, it doesn't mean we have to stay in pain and resentment. I think the way to begin healing is to understand why it happened in the first place, and to do so, we have to examine the abuser's life. In the case of my father, he was a very mentally sick individual. He had an upbringing of verbal and physical abuse at the hands of his own mother and he was never truly mentally stable. I'm not saying that is an excuse but it helps me understand why he turned out the way he did and why he did the things he did. It makes me realize it wasn't my sister's fault or my brother's fault or my fault. It wasn't even that he didn't love us. It was that he had mental disorders that led him into particular behaviors.

Why I believe that you can't forgive and forget is because forgetting about abuse is irresponsible. To forget something so important puts you into a denial system that can leave you open for a repeat situation. By remembering, you stay conscious of taking care of yourself and in time you may start to let go of some of these memories and not have them at the forefront of your mind. However, in one year or ten years you might experience anger at a parent for having abused you. Are you "bad" or "wrong" for this? NO! Unfortunately, my sister kept these thoughts and anger at the forefront of her mind which causes her to distance herself emotionally from anyone who wanted to love her and prevented her from loving others.

One of the things that has helped me is to talk to the spirit of my loved ones about my pain and feelings. I would literally just talk to thin air as if they were there. I know they are listening and looking over me which is very reassuring. I think that my loved ones would want me to get on with my life. I had to find ways to release myself from any responsibility or guilt that I was putting on myself. Without releasing these emotions, anger intensifies just as it had with Vicki. I think if you understand that God isn't to blame then why should you be to blame for what has happened. We can't stop death. As human beings, we do not have that kind of power. We are emotional beings and say and do things that are in our hearts at the time, right or wrong. You have to believe that your loved ones know your true heart and feelings now that they are deceased. I believe they can see our hearts and know our pain and that makes the relationship heal. Once my sister died, all of the bad feelings between us went away. I had the belief that she knew now who I was and that all I wanted was to love her. It took away my guilt believing that she is in Heaven with the understanding that I never intentionally meant to hurt her or cause her grief in her life. You have to believe in something. You can either believe in the guilt and anger or you can believe in the forgiveness, understanding and love. It's your choice.

Anger is a feeling that also needs to be released like all of your other emotions. Releasing anger is a crucial part of letting go. Unfortunately, many people may have been raised to think that showing your anger is wrong or disrespectful. However, anger needs to be released in order to let go of resentment and to continue experiencing other feelings such as sadness, fear, and ultimately joy. In my family, it definitely was not okay for me to show my anger. I learned that early on from my family not allowing my anger, but somehow Vicki got the message that it was okay for her to show anger all the time. It was okay for everyone else, but not for me. If I showed anger or expressed my emotions family would quit talking to me.

If anger is not dealt with it will show up in other areas of your life. These areas could be driving recklessly, unwarranted arguments, carelessness, etc... The problem often lies in the fact that many people think that expressing anger is unhealthy or dangerous. In fact, when we get to the bottom of our anger, we can usually find the root of the problem, and then begin to release it.

I learned that anger doesn't have to be explosive, and it should also not be unleashed onto others. Continual unresolved anger can keep you in a denial and guilt system. I eventually came to understand that I did not have to be happy with everyone all of the time. For me, it brought up a fear of abandonment because I felt that if I showed my anger or true feelings that people would leave me. It is normal to feel anger at someone who has left you, even if it is not his or her fault. Feelings are definitely not rational. I began to understand this the hard way because when I rationalized and justified my feelings (instead of just experiencing them) the pain just got larger. I couldn't hide any more.

I expressed to you that you have to release these emotions and feel your grief but if you are not use to doing it, how do you get started? For me I had to take actions and find people that could help me learn. I read a lot of books, listened to tapes, talked with emotionally healthy people and absorbed all the information I could. In the beginning, it was information but the more information I took in, the more I actually started to integrate it into who I was. Consider, it took several years. You just can't read a book and "poof" you're over your anger.

With each adversity, I had to remember that my loved one who had died understood that I must experience my feelings; flattering or not. I'm still alive and have to go on living my life. I knew why I was not expressing my emotions and confronting them that I was not living my life honestly. That wasn't okay with me, and I didn't want to be trapped in all of those feelings and pain for years to come. I wanted it to be over as fast as possible, so I had to get to work on the problem.

To express your anger safely and comfortably, find a place where you can be yourself or be with someone who can help guide you through your anger. This might include a therapist or a grief support group.

I remember doing activities like hitting pillows or mattresses to get my anger out or yelling at the top of my lungs to a picture of someone I was upset with. Or simply expressing to a picture of that person how I felt about what they did to me or how I felt about them dying. These activities felt silly or ridiculous at first, but I was willing to be open to it and to do whatever it took to move past all the pain. I wanted to release my feelings in private instead of taking it out on someone else in a screaming match or getting behind the wheel of a car. With my luck that would have not been a good idea!

I remember reading books on grief that seemed very clinical to me. They talked about each one of the stages of grief and I am not discounting any of the stages, but it doesn't come as a nice package like a lot of books detail. The feelings don't necessarily come in the order that is outlined in their guides. I learned that emotions come when they want to, and anger will come when it is ready.

My anger kept being put off because I had to go back to the sadness and grief due to so many deaths in such a short span of time. The anger finally came when the sadness subsided. It felt good in some ways because I knew it was an important step in moving on with my life and being complete in my grieving. In other ways, it felt scary to express these feelings. It's not that I won't always grieve for my family in some sense, but the initial impact and overwhelming feelings are not as strong now.

I knew that any unresolved feelings I may have had with my loved ones would hinder me from recovering from the impact of their deaths. Unfortunately, we are not always given the opportunity to make peace before someone dies, which was my case with most of them. There were many years of misunderstandings, fights and lies which were just too much for me to overcome. It became important for me to forgive myself, and later to learn how to forgive them.

I've learned feelings don't just go away, but they do subside over time. They will continue to cycle many times through life. After experiencing someone's death, a person may cycle through sadness, anger, joy, etc. multiple times. It would not be wrong if ten years from now you remember and re-experience those feelings and cycle through them again. If you do find a place in your heart to honestly forgive, however, it doesn't stop you from holding a person accountable for their actions.

Taking care of myself means that releasing those feelings again enables me to heal a little bit more. Not forgiving doesn't mean you can't let go and start a new relationship with an individual if that is what you choose to do. The most important thing is to release yourself from any blame, shame, or guilt. Even though I found it difficult to forgive my father, I did find a way to have a relationship with him where we could still talk. We would never have the deep intimacy of a father/daughter relationship, but at least I didn't feel I had to cut him out of my life permanently.

Dad would constantly rant in almost every phone call about all of the things that my mother had done to him. This often included making up lies and at other times telling me things I didn't need to hear. This was very difficult over the years to continue to hear these things, especially since these conversations started when I was around seven or eight. There was a period of about three years when I did not talk to my father. He didn't want anything to do with me because I had uninvited him to my high school graduation. I wanted him there, but my mother threatened me that if he showed up she would not attend. My mother had suffered greatly for many years while trying to raise Vicki and me on a single parent income. So, I felt guilty and pressured to uninvite him, and so as a consequence, my dad uninvited me from his life.

After nearly three years, we got back in touch and began slowly building a new relationship. Yet, I had to find a way that I could do that and not also be subjected to his ranting about the past. I let him know that I didn't want to hear those things, and that if he began talking about it that I would have to excuse myself from the phone. And that is exactly what I did. It wasn't the perfect relationship, but it was a way in which I could keep in communication with him and protect my own emotions at the same time.

When you do not release your emotions they are stored in your body and can add a lot of stress. This was probably why I had an ulcer at age seven! It is not surprising that illness strikes in times like these. I believe that withholding emotions creates illnesses such as stomachaches, ulcers, headaches, cancer and other ailments. When we don't release emotions our body and mind are in turmoil, which creates conflict and confusion.

Your loved one would want you to choose life and to learn from your experiences. We do not necessarily have to like how we get our lessons, however, we can choose how we will use them. Being positive does not mean you can't experience your pain through sadness, loneliness, and anger. You are entitled to all of your feelings. Even at the height of my worst feelings, I always knew that I would be okay, so I looked for a positive in the situation. I could cry, get angry, yell and then feel joy that I was alive and was able to share a part of my life with these people.

A NEW BEGINNING AND A NEW END

The next five and a half years after my sister's death I spent gathering my life back into some normality. It was not easy. All of the sudden, I found myself single and mostly alone. I spent those years in and out of several relationships as I found it was difficult for most people to understand who I was out of these circumstances that had become me.

What was interesting was that even though I had experienced a lot of grief, a lot of sadness and a lot of upheaval, I didn't take it as a negative. I kept turning each death and each event into a situation that I could grow from, but then men who entered my life were threatened by the strength that I portrayed. I think maybe they kept wondering when the other shoe was going to drop and when I was going to really get depressed. Or maybe with my luck they didn't want to be near me just in case this was a curse. I have to laugh at that thought because who could blame them.

One of the most difficult and unexpected events about having experienced these deaths was discovering I had windfalls from two of the estates. I received small amounts of money from both my mother and my sister's life insurance policies. It was a very painful and weird feeling to go to the mailbox weeks after a death and find a check for having lost your loved one. After my sister passed, I sat in the car and opened the envelope to find a dollar figure on the check I was unaccustomed to seeing. I felt an instant of joy, but it was quickly replaced by sadness because of why I had received the check. I wailed relentlessly at the top of my lungs feeling as if my heart had just been ripped out again.

I had to realize that both my mother and sister had wanted me to have this money, and as painful as it was, I came to terms with the windfall. I used the money for a good purpose, which was a down payment on a condominium. It wasn't until the first night living in my condo that the pit feeling in my stomach came rushing back at full momentum.

I sat in the dim light and admired my new home. A feeling of sadness overwhelmed me as I realized that I had my home due to my mother and sisters deaths. I wished that I could give the money back for just five minutes of their time and presence. I wanted them to see my new home and share my joy and happiness about having such a wonderful place to come home to every night. The duality of my feelings was confusing. Sadness and joy. After the overwhelming feelings subsided, I remembered that in actuality they really were with me, but in a different way now. Faith had become my oasis.

I spent exactly six years in that condo. It acted as a sanctuary for me during those years of recovery from the grief, and became a safe haven of sorts.

After experiencing five deaths in such a short period of time, I began to expect everybody around me to die. The only immediate family I had left was my brother. Whether he was the healthiest human living or not, there was a part of me that expected him to be taken away quickly after these other losses. My mother, sister, and I never thought he would live this long because of his life-long illness, yet he had outlived all of these other people. Life and death work in mysterious ways.

During this time period I truly enjoyed building my relationship with my brother John and his wife Jean. It felt good and solid for the first time in my life. Finally, two people who were away from all the dysfunction could act as a family. It was a small family, but an important one for me. I relished in those moments and days that I spent with them.

Of course, like any good novel, there would be an interruption in this glorious time. Three years after my sister's death my brother was diagnosed with liver and colon cancer and had the fight of his life on his hands. It was the fear I had always imagined that came racing back at me at full throttle.

John had become my rock and he was the only rock I had ever experienced in my family. Even after the years we spent not talking, it ended up that John and I were more alike than anyone in our family. We were the healthy ones! The ones who had made it.   Unfortunately, John would not make it much longer. He put up a three year struggle that the doctors could never imagine. He passed away May 1, 2000.

Each time I go to my brother's grave, I break down and cry as if it were the day I buried him. I don't cry much anymore, but this is a time when I release my emotions for missing him. I only get to the grave once every couple of years since I do not live in the area, but it gives me a chance to reconnect with my feelings for him. I still miss him tremendously. He had a tremendous witt and was near genious that was intriguing to be around.

Surely this was it I thought at the time. Nothing else could possibly happen. I mean my whole family had croaked! We loved that word "croaked." It was the family way of bringing laughter into the situation and it is a word I still use today as I laugh and tell people about my family. It makes them feel more at ease because if I can laugh about it maybe they can too. It is not disrespectful. It is realizing that we are called to greater purposes than what is attained on earth. I hear God laugh with me when I can find pleasure in knowing that my family is with him.

So what could possibly happen now you ask? Well, I could get cancer. Unfair you say? Impossible? Say it ain't so! Unfortunately, it was so. Almost one year after my brother passed, I was standing in the mirror and saw a black spot on my breast. It looked like dirt. I grabbed a wash cloth, ran some water on it and proceeded to start rubbing at the black mark to remove it. Unfortunately, it wasn't coming off. All the sudden I felt a lump in my throat and my heart was pounding as I took my finger and placed it on the mysterious black area and felt around. There it was. A pea sitting in my chest. "Nope, not happening to me," I quickly brushed it off. This could never happen after

I had been through so much. For Heaven's sake, I had lost my entire family and God surely wouldn't let anything else happen to me. This rationalization was spinning a mile a minute in my head.

I waited a few days as these justifications kept filtering through my thoughts, and I was even enjoying my moments of delusional denial. But then my fear set in that overpowered the denial. What if it was something? I didn't want to die. I wasn't ready, but I felt like I was being melodramatic. Who was I to think that I would have cancer and have to personally go through something where once again the attention would be on me and what I was dealing with. I began to think I was jumping to conclusions of grandeur.

I believe when a loved one dies, we are not only mourning the loss of that individual, but we are also confronted with our own mortality. I have found when someone important to us dies, we may often ask questions like: what is going to happen to me? How will I live without this person? How will my life take shape? Am I going to die? I know with the deaths I have experienced, I can admit to times of questioning the timing of my mortality.

There were days when I felt as if everyone around me was going to die. It was easy thinking this way after losing five family members in such a short time as well as my last family member, my brother. There were some days when my boyfriend was late getting home, and I would suddenly worry he was killed in an accident. I would wait by the window, pace back and forth, and call his place of work to find out when he had left. Fear can paralyze you and keep you from getting on with life if you allow it to dominate. I had to fight the fear and move on. Sometimes it meant patiently waiting it out instead of reacting by making the phone call. In time that built the trust that not everything was going to be taken from me, but however, it didn't mean that what I had today would be the same as what I have tomorrow.

Life becomes precious, yet we can't walk on eggshells. I found that embracing my fear and looking at the lessons that were given to me from these experiences awakened my strengths and tenacity for life. So, off to the doctor I went.

Unfortunately, my gynecologist was booked but his nurse practitioner could see me. She felt the spot and told me that she would be more comfortable if I went to a specialist because she felt something but wasn't sure what it was. So, I tried to stay calm as I left their office, and called the specialist to get an appointment.

The specialist felt the nodule, and said that she would be more comfortable going ahead with surgery to remove it instead of waiting to see if it grew any further. She told me that the likelihood of it being anything was a 5% chance. Well, you know my odds thus far, and sure enough, lucky me, I hit the marker. Six days later, I got the phone call while driving down the road that I had cancer sitting in my breast.

In those first few minutes after receiving the call, the one thing I did was ask God if his plan was to have me with my family. Was I to be taken too? But in my heart, I didn't feel that to be true. I felt that God was marking his plan for me, and I had to sit up and listen. Also, within those few minutes after receiving that phone call, I still remember wondering if I was going to die and if so how was I going to die and how much would I suffer. Would I have a death similar to that of any of my family members? Would I go on for years suffering or would it be a quick and timely death? Most of all, I was in shock. I was in shock that I had to ask myself these questions, and more in shock that I had to face this after everything else that had happened. We don't exactly get a say in how much is too much, however, God allows things to happen in our lives that sometimes we can't see. We may never see the reasoning at all in this lifetime, but I had to go back to my trusting skills and believe that everything was going to work out the way it was suppose to happen.

I had suspicions that something was wrong when I wasn't called back within a couple of days. Most tests don't take that long, and so I had began to suspect that they were testing and retesting to confirm. The doctor informed me that it wasn't breast cancer but the cancer in my breast was a rare form of cancer called Dermato Fibro Sarcoma, which would have to be treated similarly to breast cancer, because of the location. In the days after this announcement, I found myself dragging home after work and passing out on the couch. I would awake about 9:00pm and go back to bed. I slept like a ton of bricks had hit me. I can't even begin to tell you what I was thinking during this time because it was if I weren't thinking about anything. It was too hard. My brain hurt so I went through a lot of the motions.

During this time, I had just put my condo on the market to sell. I had been in it for six years, and it had been my cushion during all the years going through the grief. It was weird to me that right after my brother died, I suddenly had a desperate need to sell it. It was as if all my family was gone, and so now I didn't need the cushion anymore and I was ready to reach out to take a risk. I felt that that condo would hold me back from future ventures in life. It was symbolic as if I were saying, "Aha, I made it, I survived." But the timing was bad. When I got a contract on the condo, I had everything packed up ready to move, but now had an empty house with only a few pillows and blankets on the floor to sleep on. All my belongings were packed up in the garage ready to move. The floor wasn't exactly where I wanted to be sleeping after surgery, but beggars can't be choosers.

Before the initial surgery, I had met a man and we hit it off quite nicely. We were spending a lot of time together, and I had to let him know that it was cancer. To my surprise, it didn't scare him off and he seemed like he was well underway to help see me through these events. Wow, I was hopeful. Unfortunately, one day before my second surgery he broke up with me, which left me to once again fend for myself and also find a ride to my own surgery in which they would be removing a good portion of my breast. You could imagine my anguish. The feelings of loneliness hit deep because I had no family to drive me and no man to see me through it. At this point you can imagine after having lost my entire family that I became very good at coping and handling situations. It's as if I had to check it off my list and say, "next." Through all the losses I learned that I can either deal or dwell. So, I learned how to deal with these situations pretty quickly now. It's kind of sad in one way but resourceful in another way that when tragedies happen I go into overdrive and my checklist comes up in how to deal with the situation.

Over the years my relationships with friends had waned due to their lack of ability to handle listening to my circumstances (and constantly being witness to the pain) or my times of being too needy when the pain got too deep. Both circumstances reared their ugly head and had pushed most of my friends out of my life. I had become quite the lone trooper, and acted as if none of it bothered me. Co-workers were good enough to take me to the hospital and sit with me in shifts, which was one of the nicest gestures I had seen in a long time. It gave me a little hope that humans could indeed be good on occasion.

Over the next few months, I underwent two additional surgeries. After they had done the lumpectomy to remove and test the cancer, they then had to go in and do a partial mastectomy to make sure they got all of the cancer. I was terrified. All of the sudden, I was contemplating how I would explain one more travesty to someone I wanted to date. I rehearsed conversations in my head that went something like, "Well, my mother and father are dead, my sister died of AIDS, my brother died of cancer, my

Grandmother and Aunt also died leaving me without any family and oh yeah, by the way, I lost part of my breast due to cancer. Let's go out now."

If you think I'm kidding, think again. I'm not too far off base from true events, and dating during all of those years became very difficult. The first questions guys will ask you about are questions that they think are safe. Like, "Do you have any sisters or brothers?," *"Yes, dead and dead."* "Where do your parents live?", *"Hopefully in Heaven."* Well, you get my point. It could get ugly quickly and I had to learn fast what to share and with whom and how fast. The problem was that I don't have much of a dishonest bone in my body, and so when people asked me questions, I was a bit naïve in that I thought they really wanted to know or were capable of hearing the truth. Little did I know, but I would grow too.

It was always a balancing act when I met new people in deciding how much information to divulge. I learned how to hold back, and then got accused of "hiding" things. So, in many respects I felt like I couldn't win and took the attitude that if someone asked and I gave an answer that they couldn't handle, then I was better off knowing up front and not wasting my time. It seemed like a logical response anyway.

I do have to say that I had a wonderful plastic surgeon who shifted things around making my breast look almost perfect except for the huge scar in the middle of my chest. I was able to avoid having an implant. But, I was terribly lopsided as they took a good portion of my breast, which left the other one quite larger. So, I was off to my third surgery. We did a breast reduction on the normal breast to match the sizing as close as possible so I could have a somewhat normal look. I felt like my chest was a battle field, but once again, my plastic surgeon did wonders. I was amazed at his gift for being able to reconstruct me in a way that I could lead a normal life and not feel too self-conscious when someone looked at me.

Fortunately, because I caught it so early and the cancer was only in stage one, I did not have to undergo radiation or chemotherapy. Before we knew the cancer stage, however, I did have to go visit an oncologist and go through all the prepping just in case I had to begin. In those moments it felt so unreal, however, at the same time I felt so unsurprised due to everything else I had gone through over the years. I felt at this point that I had a big target on my head just asking for the next atrocity to smack me in the middle of my eyes. I had become too good at going through tragedy, and I was becoming the queen of adversity. I even had a man one time nickname me "Little JOB" after comparing me to JOB, who in the bible had everything taken away from him in one fell swoop.

Sitting in my new apartment after the surgeries, I realized that I came out of it with my life intact and well, most of my breast. It was just one more thing to integrate into the way of my life, and I found a way to add it to my repertoire. Like one wants an "adversity resume." It's okay to laugh at me because I laugh at myself. Good medicine! So, now I was on a six month regimen of mammograms and MRI's. Fun fun! But, I was alive and grateful!

THE DEMONS

When a loved one dies, we already have an enormous amount of pain without having to add guilt. When my mother died, I instantly began replaying in my head my last conversations with her, which had not been the best. Quickly, I had to stop myself from relentless guilt and realize I did everything that I could. My mother knows I love her.

After the passing of each loved one, I experienced overwhelming feelings of sadness, loss, despair, and a multitude of other emotions that felt endless. To add guilt would have put a lot of blame on me, which I didn't need and was more importantly, never warranted. These feelings are often the demons we have to overcome.

I couldn't control many of the things that happened throughout my life. It is easy to think things like, "I should have been a better daughter, (mother, father, wife, husband, son, etc...)." This does not give us a lot of room to be human. I have to remember that my loved ones are not sitting around in heaven pointing out all of the things I did wrong. That was a signal to me that I shouldn't be sitting around blaming them either. I needed to go back to remembering that although I may not be able to forgive them, I could try to understand them.

I had no idea that any of them were going to die, so it was impossible for me to say and do everything that I needed for closure. Even when someone is terminally ill and about to die, just doesn't seem to be a way to say and do everything you want. I experienced that first hand with my father and sister. Though my brother and I gave each other the opportunity to talk about his pending death, there are still things I wanted to continue to say but eventually you don't get the opportunity.

I was able to sit with my sister for several days, yet words just didn't seem to be enough. If I had done it a hundred times over it would not have felt right because the bottom line was I didn't want her to die. Believe me, it is uncomfortable and there is not a whole lot to say when you know someone is about to die. We can just reassure them of our love and their importance to us.

I had a whole different situation with my brother. John was a very unique person. First of all, he was highly intelligent. He was a self-made man, and often spent time studying any topic he could find. It was hard for him to have close friends who could understand the levels at which he operated. It was also hard finding others who could get deep into conversations about science, computers, religion and politics to keep up with his deep thoughts.

Due to his advanced mind, John was someone you could shoot the truth with, and before his death he came to me to ask me if there was anything that I needed before he died. Not many people get this opportunity. So, I gave him the opportunity back and I asked him if he needed anything from me before either of us died. Who knows, with our luck I could have been run over by a bus and killed before him. He had been told many years ago that he would die soon, but he had outlived everyone else. Why not outlive me?

John and I were able to chat, and get everything from each other that we needed emotionally and verbally before his death. It was a true gift which I encourage each person to embrace. It released a lot of feelings that I may have had to deal with if we had not had those honest conversations. Otherwise, I would have had to get into the bargaining traps. I got out of our conversations that he truly loved and valued me and that meant the world to me considering our past.

Bargaining is a guilt trap. If only I'd done 'whatever,' this would not have happened. That is a lot of responsibility and Superman could not have done it better. So, if I had remembered to take the trash out more often this wouldn't have happened? Sounds ridiculous but think about it honestly, what could I have done to prevent it? No one can take responsibility for the whole world. How long are we going to beat ourselves up? Now is the time to realize that most things in life are simply out of our control.

I remember going through my mother's house and finding these potpourri bags she had made with her old delicate lace hankies. Everyone seemed to have gotten one from her for Christmas except me. All of the sudden, I started playing this guilt routine in my head wondering what she thought of me and had I been such a terrible daughter that she didn't want to give me one of her potpourri hankies. You'd be amazed how long I spent in this guilt trap over these potpourri hankies.

I had to realize that at the time of the problems, I had to take care of my needs because no one else was capable. Unfortunately, there were times when I had to choose to not speak or see my loved ones. I realized just how human I was, which meant I had to be easy and forgiving with myself. I didn't do everything perfectly, but neither did they. We were all operating on cylinders that we knew how to work. They weren't necessarily the right ones, but they were the only ones we were given.

After a death or illness, a wide range of emotions can overwhelm us. It always amazed me how emotions would come seemingly out of nowhere causing my world to shake. In the midst of one of these heart-wrenching emotional episodes, I would experience an aftermath of fear that the pain would never diminish. I'm glad to say that the pain does get easier and lessen. However, at the time you are experiencing the pain, it can feel endless.

Since all of the deaths and my cancer situation, every time I go to the doctor there is a pang in my stomach that I cannot control and this little voice that says, "you're going to die." I hate that it happens, but the more I can recognize it as the fear that it is, the better chance I have to combat it.

Unfortunately, there are many people who have a hard time expressing their emotions, even in a time of death. Some individuals were brought up with the conditioning that you should not show your emotions, whether in public or private. This is a very unfortunate situation. Then you have people like me, who probably shared a little too much. I had to work on balancing my emotions for a really long time, and still have to make sure I keep it in check. It means sharing appropriate information and finding the right outlet to share the things you may not be able to with everyone. This will be different for each person and you have to find that balance for yourself.

You can't be fearful of expressing your emotions, but at the same time we need to make sure that we are not getting hysterical for just any reason. When we express our emotions, we are showing our vulnerabilities and this can be difficult for someone who was told while growing up to "be strong and don't cry." My mother was that way. She was the patriarch of the family, and felt that she could not let anyone see her break down and cry or suffer in any way. I believe that my brother learned that from her, and that is why it was so surprising to me when I saw him break down after my mother's death. I mean if we can't be open in front of family who can we be open with?

I remember when I got the phone call at work that my father had died, and I was standing there telling my boss that it just happened. Tears streamed down my face and while sharing my story the phone rang. In a fraction of a second, I put my show business face on, grabbed the phone, and with a clear voice answered it, "Cardiovascular and Thoracic Surgeons, how can I help you?" I thought my boss was going to fall over.

When we are vulnerable, we are truly being ourselves because we are also showing others who we are. I think back to who told me or showed me those kinds of messages, which may have been verbal or through body language but which became learned patterns. My twelve step sponsor literally taught me how to sit down and journal out these types of behaviors and cues that I picked up and also who I picked them up from. He called it an "inventory." It was very helpful because I learned that many of my behaviors that I had learned from others didn't necessarily fit into who I wanted to be. I would always ask, is this a behavior or belief I want to pass on to a child of mine? If not, I had to find a way to work through it and make the necessary changes.

Over many years, I realized that I did not have to hold on to others' beliefs forever. Especially if they didn't work for me. I created new beliefs that made it okay to show my feelings and to be vulnerable in front of others. It gave me the opportunity to open the door to many new friends and relationships and to start letting go of the demons.

THE JOURNEY TO RECOVERY

The impact of a death is overwhelming. A sense of balance left my life and getting back on track proved to be a challenging and heart-wrenching experience. I had been notified that someone I loved had just died and I was instantly struck with sadness, devastation, and a lot of fear.

Death is a great wake-up call. It reminds us that at any moment life could be all over. I found myself asking was I satisfied with everything I have done? What had I resisted because of my fear? After each death, I experienced periods of doing things that I had only talked about before because I suddenly realized I might not have a tomorrow. What was I waiting for anyway?

Fear also presents itself when we think about where our loved ones have gone. Even with the strongest faith in a God, Higher Power, or Heaven, I believe people still wonder and fear what will happen when they die. We can't fully understand or comprehend death until we experience it for ourselves. My mother always said she wasn't going to believe in little green men from Mars until she saw them. I believe this holds true for a lot of people concerning death and Heaven no matter how deep their faith.

It is difficult to put faith in something you have not seen. However, like spirituality, I believe to live with peace of mind, we have to believe in something. I am convinced of God, and that my loved ones are being taken care of and are happy in Heaven. I would not be where I am today without my faith. With everything I have gone through, I know that I can now handle anything that comes my way.

Fear is not necessarily a bad thing. Fear lets us know when we are in danger and need to protect ourselves. After my first visit to see my sister upon finding out she was ill, I was in a shopping mall when my chest suddenly felt like it was closing in on me. I began sweating and my heart rate increased. I felt like I could not get air and fear hit me as I clutched my chest. My boyfriend ran for help as my hands closed up at the fingertips and I couldn't move them. My legs were jumping like frogs. I was cold and clammy, and then suddenly my heart rate dropped.

Mentally I felt fine but I didn't understand what was happening. I had a circle of people around me wondering what was wrong. I wanted to know the same thing because felt as if I was having a stroke or something.

By the time the paramedics arrived, I was beginning to stabilize and my body was returning too normal. They told me I had experienced an anxiety attack. I could hardly believe them but as the stress began to subside my body began to return to homeostasis.

It really showed me how stress can surface when you are unaware. After this episode, I experienced several other minor instances of gasping for air. I learned from fear by embracing and accepting it instead of running from it. Facing your fears is somewhat a maturity thing. It's like being a child and being afraid of the monsters under your bed and calling in your parents to look under the bed. Now you are the responsible one and you have to begin looking under the bed. It's not always fun or easy to face them but necessary to living a functional life.

I can't exactly explain why some individuals handle crises better than others. It may be their life experiences and upbringing. Why is it that some people can get through tough situations seemingly stronger while others hit hard times? It's a question I've been asking for a long time since I had been witnessing all these adversities. It's something that I don't plan to do, but I naturally find myself watching how other people handle situations. We can learn from other people in good or bad ways.

A man I taught in a class about death said his house had not changed a bit since his wife had died over two years ago. As a result, he found his life was stagnating and he had difficulty getting on with living. He had told her children that he would split up the photographs, a task he still found impossible to do.

To cope, he dove into his work in which he traveled most of the time (out of sight, out of mind). However, it was not out of the heart, and that is where the problem begins if you are not dealing with your feelings. When you deny the situation, you are denying your feelings and the impact it has had on your life. Eventually, it will catch up to a person, and it had with this individual.

Accepting that a person is deceased doesn't mean we forget that person. There is no way we could forget the love and warmth we had for them. We will always be able to hold onto our memories, and no one can take that away from us. I hold dear to the memories even though I have dwindled down the belongings of all of my deceased to just a few boxes. I was hauling all of this stuff around and realized that much of it was just stuff and that it was okay to let it go. I kept the most important pieces to me, and that was enough.

There was a period after each death that I experienced some detachment. I think this is normal as long as it doesn't persist. I felt numb, as if I was watching all of this from the outside looking in. "How could these people have left me?" I would ask. I had to realize it was not about me. It just affected me and the detachment got me nowhere.

Also, having to deal with the people around you who don't know what to say can be added stress. I would often hear how I "should" grieve. It was easy to want to detach from the whole situation with such pressure, and so many things were overwhelming me that listening to advice became exhausting. I just wanted someone to hug me, hold me, pat me on the back and be there for me.

There are individuals who feel very uncomfortable with the topic of death, and will have difficulty expressing themselves to you. My experiences with death and my grieving weeded out those who were my true friends and those who could not be there for me. Some individuals didn't know how to be there for me, so they made themselves scarce. Fortunately, God provided me with other individuals who supported me and listened to me during my pain.

I lost many friends through this whole process. Even during the cancer I lost two friends. One of my friends (who I have to say was pretty self-absorbed anyway but she truly listened to me and most of the time gave me good advice) didn't prove to be there for me when I really needed her. During the time that I was selling my condo and sleeping on the floor right after surgery, I needed help moving two boxes down to the garage and also vacuuming the floor. My chest was bound with bandages, and I was not allowed to move heavy objects so I wouldn't rip out the stitches. I made several phone calls and could not reach anyone to help me, but I knew this friend would be home. As a matter of fact, the day before my second surgery, the partial mastectomy, I had been on the phone with her consoling her after her boyfriend had dumped her.

Now imagine that part of my breast was about to be removed, and I was trying to be a good friend and consol her through her issues while believing that just maybe we could be there for each other. The day after my surgery, when I was lying there in the middle of my floor, I called her as a last effort to get the help I needed with the boxes and the vacuuming. She had the audacity to tell me that she was too sad and upset to come over and help me. I couldn't believe my ears. I even told her that if she came over that we could talk about her pain and that being together would probably help her. But no, she was not willing to come over to help her "friend" who had just had cancer removed as well as part of her breast. That was it for me. Relationship over.

Unfortunately, I learned that humans can be very selfish and self-centered and although I know I surely had been guilty of it myself (and lost some friendships because of it), I could hardly believe this. I can only hope that I have learned to be a better friend through the experience. I do have to say that I have definitely become less tolerant in the fact that I do not have time anymore to waste not sharing my feelings about who I am. If someone doesn't like it, they need to move on. It may seem harsh, but I spent too many years playing games with my own family, and I don't want to do it with my friends. I have too much integrity to allow such dealings.

This was one of the most difficult times in my life, and I had to recognize that fact. I also had to find my own pace at which to deal with all of the changes I was experiencing. In time, I reattached to the memories with less pain and was able to talk freely about my circumstances. During the sad times, I learned how to request much-needed hugs! Often there is no need for words because the sadness is apparent.

Sadness is a genuine feeling of loss and loneliness for the grieving. It is my experience that you will have sadness at almost every stage of your grieving. When I was sad, I really understood the depth of the love that I had for my family I had lost. Memories would flood my head of the good times, bad times, and the funny times. Memories are wonderful to hold onto, however, in moments of great sadness they can bring the impact rushing back to us at full momentum.

Crying comes from our sadness, and it is a way for our body to release the pain. I feel that when we are not releasing our sadness and pain, it mounts and can develop into depression or despair. When despair is on the front-burner we may ask, "Will life ever be right again?" A cloud seems to weigh heavily on our head, making it difficult to look at the future and our hopes and dreams.

There were times when I didn't think life was ever going to be right again, but what was "right" in the first place I also had to ask. All I knew was that I had grown quite accustomed to experiencing large amounts of grief and pain and it can become quite seductive. It became what I knew how to do well and I handled it with a lot of positive attitude. I grew accustomed to handling grief and adversity. Finally, I was not only the patriarch, but one who could express her feelings (Unlike my mother, who was the patriarch in denial). I had finally arrived. However, it is hard to understand someone's positive words when we are sad, just as it is hard to understand despair when we are happy. It falls on deaf ears, and I had experienced this many times when I needed someone to understand me.

One of the problems I experienced while going through my grieving was that I would start to move out of my sadness into the anger stage and then someone else would die. So, I would then be forced back into the sadness stage. This happened four times through five deaths. Each stage of grieving will end when it is ready, and when you are ready to experience the next level of grief you will do so. I do believe that we aren't given anything that we can't handle.

I know this sounds cliché', but having been through all of this I knew that God trusted that I could handle it all. Almost weekly I hear stories of others who have survived some feat that they never imagined they could have gone through. I think we truly are capable of more than we sometimes allow ourselves to believe, and I know God isn't wrong.

I wish I could tell you there was an easy way to get through the pain quickly. Unfortunately, we have to experience the impact and everything that goes with it. Pain can rule our lives when we react to every little occurrence that interrupts it. The choice has to be made whether to play a victim or a victor. This does not mean we can't experience our pain because we have to feel all of the emotions in order to release our pain. However, fueling the pain is playing the victim.

By being the victor, we can take action to experience our pain and emotions, and therefore gain insight into how to mend our wounds instead of pouring salt into them. I don't believe that our loved ones want us sitting around feeling sorry for ourselves all of the time. We gain some knowledge from each person we meet, whether we recognize it or not. Think about what each person has brought to you, and how you use that to make a difference in your life now. Instead of choking back the tears, let them flow. Faith has to become an oasis.

People always ask me how I have become such a positive person in light of everything that has happened to me. I have to ask "why not?" It is like society expects people to cave under such circumstances, but I truly believe that without all of these losses happening to me that I wouldn't be the fun, loving, open and truly happy person I am today. It molded me, shaped who I was, and I allowed it to change me in a positive way. I simply had a decision to make. I could let this destroy me and do what my parents did and drink away the problems, or I could turn this into a situation that would change my life forever and assure me a position of greater confidence, understanding and joy. So for me, there was no decision because I wasn't willing to wallow in misery my entire life. I could sit around blaming my family or blame the deaths or the cancer, but truly, who would it hurt besides me?

THE SPIRIT WITHIN

Even having made a personal decision to choose happiness like I did, there were still moments I would ask, "How could God do this to me and the ones I love?" Questions like these are bound to present themselves when dealing with grief. Faith in God may be shaken because it's easy to feel as if this were something done to you personally.

We can't always understand why things happen the way they do. Sometimes, it may feel easier to blame someone for a death than to deal with all of the surrounding emotions. When we blame, we are able to project all of those feelings onto another energy source. If you are blaming God for "doing" this to you, you have to ask yourself what kind of God you believe in? I know I don't want a God that would purposely try to hurt me. So, I had to realize that maybe this was not about me or making me hurt, but instead about God's plans for my loved ones.

It is hard to see sometimes how a person's work can be finished on earth when they are making such an impact on our society, such as Elizabeth Glaser and her work with AIDS. This courageous woman changed peoples' perspectives on the AIDS disease, and reached out to help millions of people. When she died, it made a stronger impact on the work she did and also the need for continual persistence in the fight against AIDS. In my eyes, Elizabeth Glaser was an angel that had to endure a painful existence to teach others about the importance of life.

Even though it may seem that our loved ones die in the most unusual and cruel manner, we also have to look at the lessons brought by the tragedy. It is hard when we feel sadness and despair to believe that anything positive could come out of our loss. When I first experienced each of these deaths, it was hard to see any lessons. However, as time passed and my sadness diminished, I became aware of many important lessons I had learned from these individuals while they were alive.

At times, I feel it is unfortunate that I had to lose these people to understand the lessons, but I've learned that I can't question how the information is received. All I can do is thank God for blessing me with these wonderful individuals and the time I shared with them.

To continue on with life, I had to recognize the importance of my need for assistance, whether it is from friends, God, or best of all, both. Having faith helped me focus on my well-being and the well-being of the person I was grieving. It is difficult to deal with guilt or any other feeling alone.

I didn't always believe in God. My mother never brought me up in the church, and she generally portrayed the need for God as being weak. She never got past the experience with her own pastor, who made a sexual pass at her and assured that her children would never be given the opportunity to search for God in our own way until she was gone. It is really sad to think that she let a human experience taint her beliefs so permanently.

I wish my mother had been able to work through her pain, and maybe all of this would be different. I found that once I began working through my pain that I began experiencing this gratitude towards God, which I didn't have prior to these events. I really never believed in God before all of these events, and I often see people shun God because they think that he has left them during their trials and tribulations. For some reason, I began feeling his presence because of my circumstances, and therefore began trusting in him more and more. It didn't make sense to me then, and it really doesn't now. I just know that I had to be open to the experience for it to happen. My loved ones had departed to somewhere unknown to me and it takes a lot of faith to be comfortable with where that person might be and what is happening now. Faith is having trust in something when there is no evidence, and for the first time, I was embracing faith.

After each death I experienced, it was harder to believe I was really going through these things. If I had not established some faith, I can't say I would have handled it as well. Knowing I was being looked after by God really helped. I also knew that my family members were now my angels who were helping me by giving me strength even though I had to experience many feelings such as sadness, despair, anger and even guilt.

TAKING CARE OF YOU

I began learning through this process that I had to understand how to relax and to have help getting through this tough time. I had to learn how to let friends and people know what they could do for me to help in my healing process. Of course, I wanted to be the strong lone trooper, but it just doesn't work effectively. I had to get unafraid to ask for help, and I was only hurting myself by not allowing others to help. I learned that help may just look like silent hugs, doing laundry, cooking, talking on the phone, etc...

I also learned that people have a difficult time knowing what to do for you, even if it is nothing. They may need to know that it is impossible to read someone's mind and to know what they need or want. Death is not an easy subject for most people, and they would just as soon forget about it than have to deal with it. For those friends who do stick around and want to help, provide them with the answers on how to help.

There isn't really much you can say to a person who has lost someone. A lot of people expressed their sympathy for me, however, nothing that was said made an impact on how I felt. Don't get me wrong, it was nice knowing that people care, but the pain was so overwhelming that it was all I could feel at the time. It can be difficult expressing to others how they can be of help to us, but it is helpful just knowing they are there and aren't going to leave.

Our friends and family have the best intentions, however, they can sometimes say things that don't really help. I remember experiencing sadness, and one of my friends would say every time, "Oh, don't cry, everything will be okay."

Well, I knew everything was going to be okay, however, at the time I missed my loved one and had experienced overwhelming sadness. By her telling me this, she was taking away my feelings and making it seem that it was not all right to express myself. I know she did not mean to intentionally do that. She was just uncomfortable with my sadness because she might be uncomfortable with her own feelings. So now, when anyone says this to me, I tell him or her that I need to express my emotions. I had to be honest with them, and if they couldn't handle it they usually went away.

I realized quickly that my friends weren't always comfortable, and were having difficulty knowing how to interact with me. Letting them know what you need takes the pressure off both parties. A death is not easy for anyone involved because it means having to adjust to a new experience and lifestyle. I witnessed many people around me who had never experienced a death before became very uncomfortable around me as if I had the plague. It reminded me of a time when I visited my sister in Chicago before she was comatose. My brother-in-law and I bundled her up and got her in the wheelchair to go out to dinner per her request. I had always heard how people in wheelchairs are treated different, but didn't realize how much until this encounter.

Everyone at the restaurant couldn't take their eyes off of her, and there was this look in their face of pity, discomfort or disgust. It depended on who was looking at her, and I'm sure their own personal issues and beliefs played a role. I imagine it was hard to see such a young lady confined to a wheelchair along with a wonderment of how she got there. We are so programmed in how life "should be" that we can forget how it "can be."

Before a loved one dies, people tend to live life doing things such as working, raising children, being a husband, wife, daughter, son, participating in social activities, hobbies, etc... Life goes on as usual. We all become caught up in our daily lives, but then all of the sudden the impact of a death severely disrupts our stability. Emotions quickly rise to the surface such as panic, anger, sadness, fear, and disbelief.

Since infancy, we try to define who we are, our place within the world, and our family and friends. When a loved one dies, a piece of who we are is gone. In an instant, lives can be changed dramatically and daily rituals are no longer so easily accomplished. If you lost a spouse, you are suddenly classified as single or widowed. If you lost a child, you are suddenly childless.

Human beings get into the rituals of life. Wake up, brush your teeth, fix the kids breakfast, take them to school, go to work, come home, fix dinner, bathe the kids, tuck them in and go to bed. If you lose your child, what now happens during the times you were being their parent and following this routine that was your life? These can be some of the most painful times because trying to figure out what to do now is a difficult process. We have to re-establish who we are. We had an identity before this person entered our life, and we will again. Patience and acceptance are the keys to success.

I quickly realized how many things I used to take for granted once they were gone. I know losing most of my family in such a short time threw my identity into the wind. All of the sudden I was familyless. Is that a word? If it's not, it is now! Truly, there is a part of me that feels like an orphan, but I have also been very fortunate to have been blessed with new friends that I am turning into my family. I encourage people now to get past the small squabbles and differences because you never know what tomorrow holds. It just isn't worth it. If my sister could have just gotten past her anger, we could have spent those five years before her death discovering each other and enjoying our time. Now, it seems like such a waste.

I've also realized that obstacles in the road lead us to find paths that empower us to new destinations in life. Pity can stop an individual from getting on with life and developing healthy relationships. For instance, continually telling your story to complete strangers is one symptom. Do you grab anyone that will listen to you?

I have to say that I was guilty of this trap. Anyone that would listen was going to get the story. I had to learn how to restrain myself and learn when it was appropriate to share and when it was not. I was looking for acceptance even though I knew in my heart that these individuals could never understand the magnitude of my pain unless they had gone through it. It is common to want to let others know what you have been going through. We all need the comfort of others.

If I had continued this behavior or stayed in self-pity, these people probably would not want to be around me or be my friend anymore. We do have to be willing to help ourselves. I have been able to find individuals with similar experience so that I can share my feelings with them.

Remember that you can take this situation either as a negative or you can try to find the positive aspects that will allow you to rebuild your life. Pity will keep you in negative energy and will get you nowhere. Sharing your story in a positive way with others passes on the lessons you learned from your experience with death. Eventually, a feeling of relief will emerge. Not relief that the person has died, but a sense of gratitude that you spent time with this person and learned such wonderful things from them will emerge.

Some individuals feel relieved if they have been taking care of someone who had been ill leading up to their death. Your life has been on hold, and although you love this person very much (too much to see them suffer), you still have the hunger of life within your body. You are not responsible for your loved ones' health, therefore there is no need to feel guilt about any relief you may experience.

You do not feel relief because your loved one died, but instead you feel relief because the pain and suffering is over for them. Now, you can get on with your life and begin working through your pain. Relief is a natural feeling because we don't like to suffer. I never anticipated or wanted my sister to die, but because she was suffering so relentlessly, I was relieved when she finally passed. I found myself wishing the day would come sooner because I could not bear to think of her suffering. You are not being disrespectful to the deceased because you choose to release your pain.

My sister-in-law, who was married to my brother for thirty-one year, said that she really did not experience relief. She just wanted my brother to keep living even though she knew it was not fair to him. She explained to me that she felt like she was being selfish, but understood that most people experience this feeling. None of us want our loved one to leave us, and it is natural to want to hang on to them. She said she felt a sense of relief that he is not in pain any longer, but also said she felt a selfish feeling to want to keep him around. I believe this is normal because without him around, she had lost much of her purpose in life. I had learned this myself from wanting my own family around for my own purposes in life. It has been hard being "that person who doesn't have family." It goes beyond the "norm" and most people want to be within what society calls normal. Obviously, I stick out like a sore thumb.

We are all here on earth to learn particular lessons and to pass lessons on to others. Finding purpose in life is one of the most important tasks in developing a life you will enjoy. Without purpose in your life, it is easy to live a life "just existing" in discontent. It is normal when someone we love dies to feel that we have lost our purpose or at least question it temporarily.

I had to question myself about what "having purpose" meant to me. I believe it is not only having a reason to live, but also becoming someone that you enjoy and feel good about. Having these feelings about yourself may be a result of your accomplishments (whether physical, emotional, or spiritual) or even the hardships you have conquered. I'm proud of myself for the way I've handled my adversities. It brings me joy that I look at my situation and have found good out of the bad. It was the only way I felt that I could lead a happy life. I didn't want to resemble my mother's life which was a life of taking adversities and feeling like "poor pitiful me."

I have found after talking to people that most individuals have several purposes in life. I find that some of the purposes are about the individual, and some of the purposes are about spouses, children or other family and friends. It is wonderful to have others in our life and find purpose involving them, however, it is unhealthy to have others as your sole purpose in life. If the person dies or leaves, so does your purpose.

It is hard to imagine living without someone you love. Through my experiences in life and my loved one's deaths, I have learned many lessons. I think of these lessons as a gift to learn and pass onto others. You may not have looked at it this way but taking a positive approach to gaining a purpose in life will allow you to move forward much quicker. Staying in a negative frame of mind will only keep you down.

When we lose our purpose in our life, it is a good time to take a look at our spirituality. In the spiritual reality, we can usually find new strength and resources. When finding purpose, we also have to be resourceful. We have to take the initiative to find things in life we will enjoy, whether it is helping others, finding new hobbies or making new friends. Purpose isn't always going to find you. You are more than likely going to have to search it out.

Helping others to cope with grief has become a new purpose for me and I hope I can help others. Taking care of myself physically and emotionally has also become very important to me. Since I have lost most of my family, friends have become more important and necessary. All of these things are purposes in my life. I know it can be very painful losing someone and at times it may feel as if the pain will never decrease. I can reassure you that it will diminish, however, you have to be willing to let the process begin.

When we chose life and want to find purpose, we have to begin taking risks. It is common to feel afraid if you get close to someone else because they may die. You do not want to go through the pain again, but people will come and go throughout your entire life. When we realize this, it is a little easier to understand. However, we can never feel the impact of a loss until it has happened.

If God had intended us to go through crisis alone, then we would have been the only person on earth. There are millions of people on earth, however, and they are all here to reach out to one another and help out if we just let them. We live in a society that tells us touching is not appropriate, problems should be kept to ourselves, and that we should be brave and be able to stand on our own. But, there are times in life when we need the knowledge, touch, or the ear of someone else to help us through. Act on this and find someone.

I didn't have anything to lose, but the chance to love someone special that may bring me new powerful lessons. You may not be ready at this point, but you may again be a mom, dad, wife, or husband. New friends can help you develop a new family and support system. We always need friends, so don't shut people out because of your fears. I understand I have to embrace the life that is before me because I may not get another chance.

Right after my mother's death, I found myself somewhat detached from my memories of her. I found this to be temporary and had remembered reading about it being a normal step in the grief process, however, there are feelings of guilt, shame and sorrow that can surround it. My mother and I lived 800 miles apart, and I usually called her a couple of times a week. I really missed those phone calls after she died, and I found myself picking up the phone to call her only to realize that I could no longer physically talk to her. I would hang up in disbelief that I had just dialed her phone number.

One day I decided to pick up the phone and talk to her since I really was having difficulty feeling her presence. I just talked into the phone telling her about what I had been up to and how much I missed her. It gave me an opportunity to express how I felt, and helped me to reattach my memories. By detaching from the memories, it kept me from experiencing my feelings that were painful but necessary steps to my healing. The detachment passed with time as I expressed myself.

There were many ways I reconstructed this type of exercise. I imagined my loved one sitting in a chair or would simply look at a picture of that person. I would talk to my loved one and express how I was feeling about them dying. I would tell them everything I didn't get the opportunity to tell them when they were here. A large section of society already does this by visiting the gravesite, so our choices are not limited in how we can express ourselves to our loved ones. I found that expressing my feelings was the most important step in healing the pain and taking care of me.

It is normal and healthy to experience a vast array of feelings. Allow yourself the time to do this and be easy with yourself. Take that much needed time off and get away because grieving has no limits. This is not something that can be done in a weekend, month, or even a year, so quit feeling like you "should" be done crying. Sometimes, I did not think I was ever going to stop crying. Just when I thought I couldn't cry anymore, I would start again.

One of the most difficult aspects of grieving is that you can't always control it because you can't control your feelings. It was very difficult for me being at work some days. I would find my mind wondering onto thoughts about my family, and then the tears would come. I feel like employers should be compassionate to such circumstances, but not everyone can get this lucky.

The best thing I did was schedule a meeting with my superiors, and I explained my dilemma. They were very understanding, and I have found most of the time that if people are honest that companies want to work with you to help. We created a situation where I was able to take short breaks when I felt sadness or overwhelmed. Having a few minutes in the bathroom or away from people significantly helped me in gathering composure.

There were times, especially during the holiday seasons, that I would be in the mall with all the "happy shoppers" and families. I would begin to feel alone and start to cry. Holidays and birthdays can be extremely painful times and full of memories. In times such as this, you have to give yourself a break and figure out the best way to take care of yourself.

During holidays, I would often get invitations to other people's family events. But for me, I found that more difficult than being alone. I know that most people think that it is not good to be alone, but for me it was worse seeing a complete family unit who were happy and celebrating. It just showed me what I didn't have and would bring up sadness for me. But it doesn't necessarily mean you have to be alone either. I would sometimes find people that didn't have family in the area or couldn't make it home, and both of us would make plans to go see a movie or do our own dinner.

No one can take the place of the individual you have lost because everyone is unique. This is a time when you need family and friends around you. The void can only be lessened over time and it is easy to get into a trap of trying to fill the void with work and activities to avoid facing the reality and impact of the loss. Sometimes, I would trick myself into thinking I could get through it without feeling the pain. This is only a temporary solution.

I learned how to balance activities and quiet time to lead a healthy life. I found jumping into too much too fast just exhausted me and my emotions. However, doing too little can often keep you in your depression and sadness even longer. So, I found that pacing myself and deciding what I could and couldn't do helped. Now after some time I don't have as strong emotions being around other families celebrating the holidays. It just took time and patience and getting through my own grief.

I remember once early into the deaths being pressured by a friend to spend the holidays at her family house. I felt like I was in a pressure cooker. Being around this family brought up memories, which just made me want to cry (and believe me, people don't want their holidays ruined by an emotional crier, especially if it isn't one of their own). So, I had to choke down my emotion and tears and this was when I decided that I didn't want to put myself in that circumstance until I was more prepared to handle it. By allowing ourselves to express our emotions, we will regain our memories with less pain. Eventually, it will get easier and your memories will not be so painful.

Shortly after my mother died, I could not watch any videotapes of her, listen to audiotapes of her, or look at her old memorabilia. Experiencing all of these things was too painful, so I had to detach from a lot of my memories of her.

Now that time has passed however, I feel comfortable with these things again and find pleasure in doing them without the enormous grief I once experienced. As a matter of fact, just recently I remembered some experiences I had with my mother over twenty years ago. It had probably been over ten years since I had thought about them and it was very delightful thinking back on these memories.

When I detached myself from the memories of my mother, I took into consideration everything I was going through and didn't riddle myself with guilt or shame. I knew in my heart that I loved my mother, and she would always be in my heart and accessible whenever I chose to call on her. So, I allowed myself the period of guilt-free detachment, trusting myself and the process of life and death. We often forget we are human and you will reattach to your memories with less pain as soon as you are ready and not before.

There comes a time, as with reattachment, that you will resume your faith whether it is in a Higher Power, God, or simply life itself. By this time, you have a full understanding that you are not in this alone. God, your family, and your friends are standing next to you with an arm around you to help.

Since my family is gone, I like to imagine the whole universe embracing and supporting me. People all around the globe are experiencing grief as I have, so my collective consciousness is at work knowing I am not alone. I have faith that I will always find other people that will be of help to me along my healing journey.

For me, ultimately, I know that I am being protected and that the deaths of my loved ones were not about me. They just affected me. However, at the same time, there have been many lessons for me to learn. With this understanding, I can resume any faith that I might have lost along the way. It was hard sometimes to believe that "someone up there" was doing this "to me." I must have been very important to have so much attention and it is kind of laughable when you think about it in this perspective.

I may not know until my own death all of the answers, however, I have found peace that me and my loved ones are being taken care of by God. With this in mind, I was able to get on with my life while taking with me my new lessons.

Life has started taking on new meaning for me. I shared life with my deceased loved ones, who influenced me greatly. Whether good or bad, I learned who to be and who I didn't want to become. I found that with my new life I began resuming activities that I was once involved in and also created new ones. My loved ones are now safe and are watching over me. It's like I have a team of cheerleaders!

I have enjoyed carrying those lessons to new heights by living and passing it along. You can meet new people knowing that your loved one will never be replaced in your heart, but instead that they are guiding people to help you learn new lessons that will continue your growth process. We can only be responsible for ourselves and you choose how you want to live life.

Death is not a good excuse to put off life because of your own fears. I had to quickly get how to not use death as an excuse that would hold me back. Of course, I knew I would experience a lot of pain and other emotions, but I did not want my grief to be exactly the same five years from now. I realized that it could be if you I did not work on experiencing and expressing the emotions and letting go.

To continue, you have to implement your lessons and your new purposes for life. How can you implement these lessons? By living them. Are you practicing what you preach? Ask yourself what you've learned from the experience of death. Now make a list of your daily activities and behaviors. Do they make you happy? If not, I think the next question is how can I make changes to improve my consciousness and quality of life.

With all of this behind me and a new strength that is immeasurable, I understand I was never really alone. A teacher explained to me that it took me getting to the point where I felt so lonely in the world to realize that I really was not alone.

Six people I loved in very different ways are now gone from my life. I look forward to the day I can meet with them, wherever and whenever that may be. I believe that they all provided me with a lot of lessons before and after their deaths that I can now be grateful for. However, it doesn't take away the pain completely. I miss them.

Sometimes our purpose in life is made all too obvious and other times we have to search for it. My messages are coming loud and clear. Though my blood relations on this earth are at an end, my connections with the earth's vast array of souls are expanding. Through the grief, there is happiness. This is my message to you!

End Note

I have recently gone through two additional surgeries due to a pre-cancer in a new location. I continue the fight and am determined that these things will not bring me down, but will continually push me to live life without fear and resolve. And having this knowledge about my health makes me want to live all the more boldly, happily, stronger and self-aware. "Keep on plugging along" as my brother would say!

Printed in the United States
92502LV00001B/178-195/A